COGNITIVE BEHAVIORAL THERAPY MADE SIMPLE

By

Gary Scott

TABLE OF CONTENTS

INTRODUCTION

In the way we live and think, everything is dedicated to material pleasure. We consider objects to be of utmost importance and materialistically devote ourselves to whatever makes us happy, famous and popular. Even though all this comes from our mind, we are so totally preoccupied with the external objects themselves that we never look within, we never question what makes them so appealing.

However, this mind is an integral part of us; as long as we exist, our mind is there within us. Thus we are always up and down; it is not our body that goes up and down; it is our mind, whose way of functioning we do not understand. Therefore, sometimes you have to examine yourself; not just your body but your mind, which is the thing that is telling you what to do. You have to know your psychology, or, in religious terminology, perhaps, your inner nature. But no matter what you call it, you have to know it.

Don't think that examining and knowing the nature of your mind is only an Eastern trip. That's a wrong conception; it's not an Eastern trip, it's your trip. How can you separate your body or the picture you have of yourself, from your mind? You can't say, "I have the power to separate my body from my mind." That's impossible. You think you are a free person in the world, enjoying everything. That's what you think, but you are not free. I'm not saying that you are under the control of someone else; it's your attachment, your uncontrolled mind that you are oppressed by. If you can discover how it oppresses you, the uncontrolled mind will disappear automatically. Thus knowing your own mind is the solution for your mental problems.

One day the world is so beautiful; the next day it is so bad. How can you say that! Scientifically the world can't change radically like that. It's merely your mind that makes this happen. Don't think that this is religious dogma; our going up and down is not religious dogma. I'm not talking about religion; I'm talking about the way you lead your life, which is what sends you up-down. The people and the environment don't change radically; the changes are in your own mind. Surely you can understand that—it's so simple.

Similarly, one person thinks that the world is beautiful and people are lovely and kind, but another thinks that everything and everyone is horrible. Who is right? How do you explain that scientifically? It's just the individual mind's projection of the sense world. Hence you feel, "Today is like this, tomorrow is like that; this man is like this; that woman is like that. Even seeing somebody beautiful is somehow a creation of your mind.

Also, you should not expect material objects to satisfy you and make your life perfect. How can you be satisfied with even vast amounts of material objects?

How can you be happy with sleeping with hundreds of different people? Satisfaction comes from the mind. Your dissatisfied mind wanting to keep changing from one person to another, from one thing to another, can never satisfy you. All of this is in your mind only.

So you see, if you don't know your own psychology, you might ignore what's going on in your mind until it breaks down and you go completely crazy. People go mad through a lack of inner wisdom, the ability to examine their own minds. They cannot explain themselves to themselves; they don't know how to talk to themselves. They are not aware of their inner "world." Self-analysis, therefore, it is necessary as well as the ability to examine your mental attitudes. However, you don't need to embark on some emotional or religious journey to explore yourself. Some people, however, think that this kind of self-analysis is something spiritual or religious, although if you want to be happy, you do have to check the way you lead your life. Your mind can become "your religion."

You should be able to relax and face problems with positivity. Just be conscious of them and their origin, knowing their root. Introduce them to yourself. Then the problem will automatically ease. It's not too hard if you want it, be conscious that you have a mind. You cannot deny your mind. Therefore, treat yourself wisely and try to discover the real source of satisfaction.

When you were a child, you may have loved and

craved things like sweets or toys or things that you couldn't afford, thinking "When I'm old like my parents, I'll have all the things I want, and then I'll be happy." Now you may have the things you were craving for, but you are still not satisfied and perhaps want more or different things you may or may not be able to afford. Therefore, you will search for other sources of happiness, but in the end, you would still be dissatisfied with something. Then,what is satisfaction? Examine your life from childhood to the present—meditate. You have changed your mind several times and not truly understood what makes you happy and you may feel somehow lost if you can not find your goals in life. Therefore, Lord Buddha is saying that you only have to know who you are, how you exist; that's all. You don't have to do anything. Just understand your mind: how it works; how attachment and desire arise; how lack of knowledge results; where the emotions come from. It is sufficient to know the nature of all that; just that gives so much happiness and peace. Your life changes completely; everything gets turned upside down; what you interpreted as horrible becomes beautiful. It's truly possible.

I'm sure that if I told you that all you were living for was chocolate and ice cream, you'd think I was crazy. No, no, no, your arrogant mind would say. But look deeper into your life's purpose. What are you here for? To gain a good reputation or to collect material things? Or maybe to try to look good to others? I'm not exaggerating— check for yourselves, then you'll see. Through examination, you can realize that if your entire life is dedicated to seeking happiness through superficial things there is no significance in your being a human. Birds and dogs have the same kind of attitude to life. If you think you're intelligent you should dedicate your life to goals higher than those of chickens!

I'm not dictating your life for you, but It's much better to have an integrated experience than to live in a mental disorder. Otherwise, your life is not worthwhile, not beneficial to yourself or others. Ask yourself what you are living for—for chocolate? For steak? Perhaps for education. But that also comes from the mind. Without the soul, what is knowledge, what is philosophy? A philosophy is somebody's way of thinking, thoughts put together in a certain way. Without the mind there's no philosophy no doctrine, no university subjects. These things are mind-made.

How to check the mind? Just watch how it perceives or interprets any object that it makes contacts with. What feeling—comfortable or uncomfortable is. Then you ask yourself, "When I recognize this feeling or emotion, I react in a certain way. This is how to check the mind; that's all; it's straightforward.

When you have checked your own mind correctly, you may stop blaming others, recognizing that actions come from yourself. When you are preoccupied with the material, external objects, you always blame them and others for your problems. Then you become miserable because you project that view onto external phenomena instead of seeing their reality. So you can realize your fade-conception view—the attitude, or nature, of your own mind.

You might think that this is all very new for you, but it's not. Whenever you are going to do anything, first you check whether to do it or not and then make your decision. Since you do this already, I'm not giving you something new; the difference is that you are not doing it enough. You have to do more checking. To do this you don't have to sit in some corner on your own—you can be checking your mind all the time, even while talking or working with other people. Also, you shouldn't think that examining the mind is something only for those who are abroad. Don't think that way.

You should also realize that the nature of the mind is different from that of the mesh and bone of this physical body. The mind is like a mirror, reflecting everything without discrimination. If you have understanding-wisdom, you will control the sort of reflections you allow in your mind-mirror. If you ignore what is happening in your mind, it will reflect all negative things that would make you psychologically ill.

Your checking-wisdom should distinguish between beneficial reflections and those that bring psychological problems. Eventually, when you realize the nature of subject and object, all your questions will dissolve.

Some people think they are religious, but what is spiritual? If you are not examining your own nature, not gaining knowledge-wisdom, in what way are you religious? Just the idea that you are religious—I am Buddhist, Jewish—does not help at all. It does not help you; it does not help others. If you have knowledge-wisdom, you can help others.

The most significant problems of humanity are psychological, not material. From birth to death, people are continuously under the control of their mental sufferings. Some people never check themselves when things are going well, but when something goes wrong—an accident or some other terrible experience—they immediately say, God, please help me. They call themselves religious, but they're aren't. In happiness or sorrow, a severe practitioner maintains constant awareness of God and his nature. You're not realistic or even remotely religious if you forget yourself when you are having a good time, surrounded by materialistic things and preoccupied with worldly sense pleasures, and turn to God only when something awful happens. That doesn't help.

No matter which of the many world religions we consider, their interpretation of God or Buddha or whatever is simply words and mind; only these two. Therefore words don't matter so much. What you have to realize is that everything—good and evil; all kinds of philosophies and doctrines—comes from mind. The mind is mighty; therefore it requires strong direction. A powerful jet plane needs a good pilot; your mind-pilot should be wisdom understanding the nature of it. Then powerful energy can directed to benefit your life instead of being allowed to run uncontrollably like a mad elephant, destroying yourself and others.

It's widely recognized that a few sessions of cognitive-behavioral therapy (or CBT) can be beneficial in treating the anxiety and depression that so many people experience. However, many people don't have access to a CBT therapist—maybe none are close by, or they're not in the person's insurance network, or they're prohibitively expensive. It can also be challenging to take time off from paid work or childcare every week to see a therapist.

If you're interested in CBT for anxiety or depression and you aren't able to see a CBT therapist, take heart—you may not need to. There are multiple options for doing CBT without a therapist, including self-help books and Internet-based treatment. Many studies have shown that self-directed CBT can be handy.

For example, a review of 33 studies found that self-help treatment led to significant reductions in anxiety; another review of 34 studies on depression found similar benefits of self-directed therapy, mainly when the treatments used CBT techniques. Both reports found that, on average, the self-help treatments were moderately helpful. In other words, people who did the therapy felt substantially better—maybe not like "a new person," but a noticeably less anxious or depressed version of themselves.

Data from these studies also suggest that people who do self-help CBT for anxiety and depression tend to hold on to their progress over time, which is very encouraging. One of the primary goals of CBT is for you to "become your own therapist" by learning skills that you can continue to practice after you've ended treatment. These studies show that people who learn CBT skills on their own can use these skills to keep feeling well.

Does this mean the end for therapists? Certainly not. One of the other findings from the studies above is that CBT with a therapist tends to be more effective than self-help CBT, so there can be an additional advantage to working with someone directly. Self-help treatment can also be done with a limited amount of input from a professional—for example, a brief phone call each week—which can provide an extra boost compared to self-help alone. I suspect that the added benefit from working with a therapist comes not only from having the input of an expert but also from having a caring person's consistent encouragement.

CBT is part of a movement toward stepped care, in which the goal is to match the intensity of treatment to a person's needs. Someone who is severely depressed and barely able to get out of bed is probably not a good match for self-directed CBT, and likely will need one-on-one treatment with a professional. On the other end of the spectrum, a person with mild to moderate anxiety or depression which is generally able to function well may be the right candidate for a less intense option like a book on CBT.

SELF-THERAPY

Because there are so many different ways of going about self-therapy – from CBT to Rational Emotive Behavior Therapy (REBT), IFS, and more, there are many different tips out there on how best to go about doing self-therapy.

Start by thinking about what you'd like to achieve. Are you hoping to learn techniques for managing anxiety? Are you looking to nip negative thoughts in the bud? Do you want to work on developing some positive current behaviors? There's no 'right' answer. Clarifying your overarching goal will simply make your different objectives easier to understand.

Study your feelings and behaviors more closely. Take a closer look at how your problem is presenting. Are you hoping to deal with a behavioral problem, like avoidance or coping behaviors? Or are you wanting to target unwanted feelings, like social anxiety or stress?

Studying your behaviors or emotions at a more in-depth level can involve describing your feeling or action, recalling times that you thought or acted a certain way and keeping a record of when and where these feelings or behaviours tend to show up.

Ask yourself: what were you thinking at that precise moment? How intense was the atmosphere? Where were you and who was there? Are there certain situations that lead to the problem?

Identify and explore any associated self-talk and thoughts.

Very often, irrational or unhelpful cognitive mental processes are behind unwanted feelings and behaviors. Stress, anxiety, depression, and even relationship difficulties can often be addressed by identifying the negative self-talk or distortions that go on in our heads.

Challenge your irrational thoughts and internal dialogue

Regardless of which direction you choose to take your self-therapy, the goal is to feel more positive. We can do this much more effectively by addressing the root cause of the problem, which a lot of medications don't do.

As an example, Sarah is given feedback on a work task by her boss. Instead of allowing herself to think negatively (e.g. "I'm not good enough"), she replaces this with a more objective, rational thought. Instead, she thinks: "My boss sees my full potential, and I'm excited to grow and realize that potential."

Practice

Every day, we face triggers and external events that

we have no control over. As we practice, develop, and strengthen our rational and positive thought processes, we get better at managing our responses to them. Reward yourself with something you enjoy doing for keeping up the good work.

Self-Therapy questions

Self-therapy questions aim to probe a little deeper into the nature of whatever anxiety, depression, or emotional problems you might be experiencing.

These can take many different forms and may entail part of a much longer-term process.

Self-therapy questions require nothing more than something to write with, but keeping your answers on hand can be very helpful over the long term. You or your patients may find that being as honest as possible while answering makes for more powerful reflection at later points in time.

The Cycle of Anxiety Worksheet and questions

This worksheet and set of questions are best used together. The Cycle of Anxiety worksheet is designed to help those of us with anxiety understand how the symptoms often lead us to engage in avoidance behaviors. Because many therapeutic interventions (such as CBT) attempt to deal with anxiety by 'breaking the cycle,' the illustration can be helpful to visualize, understand, and target the source of our concern.

As part of self-therapy, you can use the Cycle illustration to introduce yourself or your client to the concept of how feedback and reinforcement contribute to the recurrence of avoidance behaviors.

This activity can help facilitate an understanding of why it's often essential to tackle the source of these negative emotions head-on when they occur. As a therapist, it is often not possible to be around when your client experiences external anxiety-inducing triggers, and this worksheet is very handy for them to have on hand.

The questions accompanying the worksheet help you or your client make the Cycle more meaningful, and include the following:

• What are three things that trigger your anxiety?

• What are three physical symptoms that you experience when you feel anxious?

• What are three thoughts you tend to have when you feel anxious?

• What are three things you do to cope when you are anxious?

By asking yourself these questions, you can develop a better sense of what triggers your anxiety, how it manifests physically and mentally, and the avoidance behaviors you commonly exhibit.

Questions for Challenging Negative Thoughts

Anxiety and depression often come together, being brought about by negative thought processes. These questions are designed to help you or someone you know to challenge these maladaptive thoughts and help you reassess them. Ideally, they should provide an alternative perspective and help you cope with or reframe the situation.

• Is there substantial evidence for my thought?

• Is there evidence contrary to my thought?

• Am I attempting to interpret this situation without all the evidence?

• What would a friend think about this situation?

• If I look at the situation positively, how is it different?

• Will this matter a year from now? How about five years from now?

Challenging our subjective or potentially distorted thinking patterns is a logical next step to being able to identify and recognize them, which the Cycle of Anxiety exercise above helps with. The questions can be very helpful if a client or you yourself realize that you might be catastrophizing, overgeneralizing, or magnifying/minimizing the importance of certain situations.

Questions for Cognitive Distortion

These questions are especially useful because they can be easily adapted to meet a whole range of different levels and stages of emotion. They are aimed at helping you or your client understand that the worst possible solution is not always right.

When you feel that you are at risk of catastrophizing when you feel the onset of either anxiety or an unnaturally low mood, ask yourself:

• What are you worried about?

• How likely is it that your worry will come true? Give examples of past experiences, or other evidence, to support your answer.

• If your worry does come true, what's the worst that could happen?

• If your worry does come true, what is most likely to happen?

• If your worry comes true, what are the chances you'll be okay...

- In one week? _____%
- In one month? _____%
- In one year? _____%

Discovering your Inner Critic

These questions are designed to be self-administered. The test itself shouldn't take longer than 8 minutes, and the results will be most helpful to you if you answer them using your first reaction.

Based on the answers you give, you will ideally be able to get some understanding of the internal parts of yourself that give you unnecessary negative messages.

Each question is answered on a five-point scale ranging from Never to Always.

• I set extremely high standards for myself.

Never / Seldom / Sometimes / Frequently / Always

• I push myself to work very hard so I can achieve my goals.

Never / Seldom / Sometimes / Frequently / Always

• When I think of trying something new and challenging, I give up before I begin.

Never / Seldom / Sometimes / Frequently / Always

• I have a hard time feeling OK about myself when I'm not acting in accordance with my childhood programming.

Never / Seldom / Sometimes / Frequently / Always

• It is hard for me to start on new projects because it is unacceptable to make mistakes even when I am just learning.

Never / Seldom / Sometimes / Frequently / Always

• I am troubled by something I have done that I cannot forgive myself for.

Never / Seldom / Sometimes / Frequently / Always

Using Self-Therapy for Anxiety

Unpredictability is part of the very nature of anxiety. Triggers can be internal or external, and it's easy to feel overwhelmed fairly quickly. As mentioned, not everyone can access a therapist instantly, so guided self-therapy can be incredibly helpful for dealing with daily occurrences that might lead to moderate or mild anxiety.

How does self-therapy work for anxiety?

Often, self-therapy is used as part of a stepped-care model. This means it is considered a low-intensity treatment which individuals with anxiety can do without therapeutic intervention. At the same time, carrying out self-therapy for anxiety can help us understand if a more high-intensity approach is required, while also being a useful tool to use alongside one-on-one therapy.

There are many different forms of self-therapy for

anxiety and work-related stress including, but not limited to:

• Psychoeducation – resources to help you understand the nature of anxiety and the vicious Cycle of Anxiety are frequently found with self-therapy worksheets, questions, and exercises. We've given some examples above, and these sheets also provide valuable information about what treatments you or your client may be interested in pursuing;

• Relaxation – of course, relaxation is a huge part of treating anxiety. Meditations, guided breathing, music, exercise, and more can be part of self-therapy, and you can find more activities for targeting anxiety;

• Cognitive Restructuring – the 'Challenging Negative Thoughts' exercise above is a brilliant example of how cognitive distortions can contribute to anxiety and stress as well as depression. Cognitive restructuring involves identifying and changing the maladaptive thought processes underpinning negative emotions and symptoms;

• Anxiety Management Techniques – typically used alongside cognitive restructuring and relaxation, these can include 'grab-and-go' self-therapy techniques that work well in everyday life. These can include positive self-talk, grounding techniques, and related exercises, some of which we've included below in our worksheets section.

Self-Therapy for Depression

In a nutshell, self-therapy for depression uses a lot of the same techniques and approaches. Most self-therapy approaches to handling depression use CBT techniques to identify, combat, and change negative thoughts.

Individuals can easily learn to develop Cognitive Behavioural Therapy skills, and when self-directed, these can help to somewhat reduce feelings of anxiety as well – the two are often found together.

Neuroimaging research also provides evidence to suggest that CBT helps to reduce activity in our self-referential medial prefrontal cortex, which is typically 'on' when we're having negative self-thoughts.

OCD, Social Anxiety and Self-Therapy

Because both social anxiety and obsessive-compulsive disorder (OCD) are related to feelings of anxiety, self-therapy is frequently used as a means of addressing both. In fact, just under a quarter of those found to have OCD are also diagnosed with social anxiety.

Self-therapy, in this case, will often involve identifying the anxious 'parts' of our psyche that are driving obsessive thoughts, compulsive behavior, or feelings of fear relating to social situations.

Social anxiety can often drive behaviors, particularly avoidance-related behaviors, and self-therapy directed at treating it often starts with psychoeducation.

Research points towards the effectiveness, in particular, of cognitive-behavioral bibliotherapy and internet-based programs for individuals with social anxiety. Even more encouragingly, these improvements showed signs of having endured in follow-up trials a year later.

Gratitude Exercises Worksheet

You can easily use this worksheet yourself, or to help your clients learn how to practice gratitude by getting involved in several activities:

Journaling: By taking time each day to record a few nice things that happened, you can reflect on these if and when you feel anxious or depressed.

Letter Writing: Composing letters to those who you're thankful for and getting it down on paper can really trigger some strong positive emotions. The worksheet guides you through this.

Expanding on this theme, other exercises in the worksheet include:

- Visiting those you appreciate, or those who have had a big positive impact on your life;
- Saying 'Thank You' and looking for reasons to

thank people;

- Gratitude Walks, during which we can focus externally rather than internally, looking around us at things that make us feel appreciative.

The Internal Family Systems Model (IFS) and Self-Therapy

The Internal Family Systems (IFS) Model is a type of psychotherapy based on the concept that our psyches comprise multiple subpersonalities. These multiple separate parts, which can be thought of as painful emotions, exist within our mental systems and can be at conflict with one another, and with our spiritual center, the Self.

Our Inner Parts

Each subpersonality has a distinct set of motivations, goals, feelings, and emotions, such as 'the angry part', 'the loving caretaker', 'the inner critic' and more.

Developed by Dr. Richard Schwartz, IFS therapy allows us to recognize, target, and transform these different parts into inner strengths. In other words, resources of strength, love, and freedom that we can draw on to deal with depression, anxiety, and other manifestations of imbalance between our 'inner parts'.

The ultimate goal of IFS in self-therapy is to engage directly with these facets of our psyche and heal them in order to access the Self, a source of creativity, compassion, clarity, and courage.

According to the IFS Model, we experience our inner parts through our feelings, thoughts, as well as through physical symptoms such as anxiety and depression. Some are proactive, while others can be 'exiled' – meaning they can't carry out their intended roles of acting to help you.

Protective inner 'parts'

The Managers – these proactive 'organizer' parts of our psyche strive to keep balance in our systems by keeping feelings associated with 'exiled' parts in check. 'Manager' parts help us control our behavior in different situations by avoiding risks and worry, by evaluating ourselves and others, and related protective behaviors.

The Firefighters – more reactive than 'Managers', these inner parts aim to distract you or dissociate from the exiled parts of your psyche when these come into play. Physically, they can be felt as anxiety, hypervigilance, or related symptoms such as panic and digestive problems.

Exiles

A detailed descriptions suggest, 'Exiles' are young parts or the psyche that have become separated from the rest of our systems for their own, or our, protection.

Traumatic, difficult, or painful experiences may have lead to this isolation, and these parts carry the feelings and sensations of these past experiences. When situational factors, or the IFS psychotherapy process are used to access these 'exiled' parts, they can lead us to feel extreme emotions in an attempt to be heard and attended to.

MOST EFFECTIVE TOOLS OF CBT THERAPY

The basic idea of cognitive behavioral therapy is that your thinking determines your quality of life. If you change your thinking, you will improve your life. External factors influence your life to some degree, but it is mostly how you interpret external factors that has the greatest impact.

If you feel the need to be perfect, small disappointments will feel like major failures. If you dwell on your worries or fears, you will eventually feel overwhelmed. If you hold on to disappointments or resentments, you will sap the joy out of life. How you choose to interpret events, and your ability to reframe them, is the power of mind over mood.

Ask your therapist or doctor if cognitive therapy is right for you. These techniques can complement the work you do with your therapist or doctor, but they are best done in combination with professional guidance.

What is Cognitive Behavioral Therapy?

It is a step-by-step method for identifying your negative thinking and replacing it with healthier thinking. It changes your inner dialogue. Numerous studies have shown that cognitive behavioral therapy is effective for treating anxiety, depression and addiction.

Negative Thinking

Negative thinking leads to negative consequences. It is based on false beliefs or on a few selective facts, and it ignores important facts that would lead to better consequences. Negative thinking is usually rigid, absolute, and not supported by most of the facts.

When your thinking is rigid and absolute, you tend to take an all-or-nothing approach and you are resistant to change. For example, you may think that you are a failure at everything, and you may be resistant to hearing encouraging advice from your friends.

Sometimes it's hard to recognize negative thinking. Cognitive therapy is designed to help you recognize your negative thinking and discover healthier thinking patterns.

Common Negative Thinking Patterns

1. *All-or-Nothing Thinking:* "I have to do things perfectly, and anything less is a failure."

2. *Focusing on the Negatives:* "Nothing goes my way. It feels like one disappointment after another."

3. *Negative Self-Labeling:* "I'm a failure. If people knew the real me, they wouldn't like me. I am flawed."

4. *Catastrophizing:* "If something is going to happen,

it'll probably be the worst-case scenario."

5. *Excessive Need for Approval:* "I can only be happy if people like me. If someone is upset, it's probably my fault."

6. *Mind Reading:* "I can tell people don't like me because of the way they behave."

7. *Should Statements:* "People should be fair, and when they are not fair they should be punished."

8. *Disqualifying the Present:* "I'll relax later. But first I have to rush to finish this."

9. *Dwelling on the Past:* "If I dwell on why I'm unhappy and what went wrong, maybe I'll feel better."

10. *Pessimism:* "Life is a struggle. I don't think we are meant to be happy. I don't trust people who are happy. If something good happens in my life, I usually have to pay for it with something bad."

Causes of Negative Thinking

Negative thinking is learned thinking. If you see important people in your life using negative thinking, it will start to seem normal, you won't question if it is healthy or not or where it came from.

Negative thinking turns into automatic thinking through repetition. By the time you are independent enough to do your own thinking, you may have been exposed to numerous examples of negative thinking. Without even questioning it, you will automatically assume that you are wrong, or a failure, or disliked.

Automatic thinking is helpful in everyday life, because you have so many minor decisions to make that you can't take time to ponder every choice. It allows you to navigate life efficiently. Automatic thinking can also be unhelpful if your assumptions are false. If you have absorbed a negative way of thinking, then you will often come to the wrong conclusions.

With cognitive behavioral therapy, you can unlearn what you knew and learn new skills and new ways of thinking that can lead you to a better life.

Consequences of Negative Thinking

The consequences of negative thinking are cumulative. One negative thought piled on top of another starts to take a toll on how you view yourself and your future.

If you think that any mistake is a failure, this all-or-nothing thinking can lead to anxiety. You worry that any mistake may expose you to criticism or judgment. Therefore you don't give yourself permission to relax and let down your guard.

If you think that you are broken, unfixable, or unlikeable, this negative self-labelling can lead to depression. You are trapped by your own unrealistic view of yourself. Feeling trapped is one of the common causes of depression.

Negative thinking that can lead to anxiety or depression can also lead to addiction, because anxiety and depression feel so uncomfortable that you may turn to drugs or alcohol to escape.

Negative thinking not only leads to unhappiness, it is also an obstacle to self-change. When you think in an all-or-nothing way, then the idea of change feels like an overwhelming challenge. You can't see the small steps, and you don't have the energy to take big steps, therefore you feel stuck.

CBT Worksheets (Thought Record)

A CBT Worksheet (also called a Thought Record) helps you reflect on your way of thinking. A basic tool of cognitive therapy, it is a series of questions that lead you step-by-step through the process of identifying your negative thinking and changing it.

This worksheet gives you a chance to analyse your thinking and actions after the fact has happened, so that strong emotions won't affect you during the process and you can easily identify your negative thinking.

A Thought Record helps you see what your negative thought are based on, what might have triggered it and finding ways to deal with the problem and find healthier ways of interpreting the facts.

CBT Worksheet/Thought Record Template

1. *The trigger:* Briefly describe the situation that led to your unpleasant feelings. This will help you remember the situation later if you review your notes.

2. *Initial thought:* What thought first crossed your mind? This was probably a subconscious or automatic thought that you have had before.

3. *Consequences:* Why do you want to change this thinking? What will be the consequences if you don't change? Look at the psychological, physical, professional, and relationship consequences.

4. *Challenge your initial thought:* How successful has this thinking been for you in the past? What facts do you have that support or challenge your initial thought? What strengths do you have that you may be overlooking? What advice would you give someone else in the same situation?

5. [Optional] *Negative thinking:* Summarize the kind of negative thinking behind your initial thought. Identify one or more of the basic types of negative thinking, for example all-or-nothing, focusing on the negatives, catastrophizing, or negative self-labelling.

6. [Optional] *Origin:* When did you first have initial thoughts like this? How deep do the roots go? Do you know anyone else who thinks like this? How successful has this thinking been for them?

7. *Alternative thinking:* Now that you understand your negative thinking, how could you have handled the situation differently?

8. *Positive thinking and affirmation:* Write down an affirmation, in a positive form, that reflects your healthier approach. Choose something that you can use as a reminder.

9. *Action plan:* What can you do if this situation arises again? How can you prepare for the situation? Write a list of strengths you bring to the situation. Knowing your tendencies, what can you do if you fall back on old habits?

10. *Improvement:* Do you feel slightly better or more optimistic? This step reinforces the idea that if you change your thinking, you will change your life.

How Effective is Cognitive Behavioral Therapy?

Cognitive behavioral therapy has been proven to be more effective than other forms of psychotherapy for anxiety and depression, as it helps to change the wiring of your brain. When you challenge your negative thinking, you create new neural pathways. The more you practice your new way of thinking, the more you strengthen those pathways.

MRI studies have confirmed that cognitive therapy changes the wiring of your brain and this is why the benefits of cognitive behavioral therapy are not just temporary.

The principles of cognitive behavioral therapy are so sound that it can be used effectively in a number of settings. Cognitive behavioral therapy has been shown to be effective when delivered in primary care, via computer, and through internet-based self-help programs.

Behavioral Therapy

CBT is a combination of two forms of therapy: cognitive and behavioral therapy. Behavioral therapy is sometimes used initially with individuals who are too anxious or too depressed to even acknowledge that their thinking is part of the problem.

Behavioral therapy encourages you to try simple tasks and as you succeed, you gradually improve your belief in yourself. Once you see that you can change your behavior, you may be more willing to change your thinking. In most cases, individuals who are ready to change are encouraged to start directly with cognitive therapy rather than begin with behavioral therapy.

History of Cognitive Behavioral Therapy

In the 1950s, American psychologist Albert Ellis introduced Rational Therapy in which people were taught the A-B-C-D approach for dealing with uncomfortable situations. When a person is confronted with an adversity (A) their beliefs (B) will influence the way they respond to that adversity and lead to emotional and behavioral consequences (C).

If the beliefs (B) are rigid, absolute, and unrealistic, the consequences (C) will likely be self-defeating and destructive. If the beliefs (B) are flexible and constructive, the consequences (C) will likely be positive. People can change their thinking and their lives by disputing (D) and challenging their beliefs.

Rational therapy was partly developed as a reaction to psychoanalysis, which was considered inefficient because individuals went through years of therapy, but were not explicitly directed to change their thinking. Psychoanalysis was based on the approach that understanding your subconscious thoughts would eventually lead to self-change. Rational therapy takes a more directive approach. You are encouraged to challenge your beliefs in order to achieve faster and more efficient change.

In the 1960s, American psychiatrist Aaron T. Beck introduced Cognitive Behavioral Therapy partly based on the ideas of Albert Ellis and used it as a treatment for depression. Beck developed the idea of the thought record, in which individuals could challenge their thinking through writing their thoughts down and looking for healthier ways of thinking. He also developed self-reporting measures for anxiety and depression including the Beck Anxiety Inventory (BAI) and the Beck Depression Inventory (BDI).

Ineffective ways people try to stop negative thinking

People often try many different ways to get rid of their negative thoughts, including distractions or diversions, only to later mentally beat themselves up for being still stuck in their negativity. It can feel like a real internal battle.

Key one – recognise & step back from negative thought patterns

Negative thought patterns are repetitive, unhelpful thoughts. They directly cause what we could describe as 'negative' (unwanted or unpleasant) emotions like anxiety, depression, stress, fear, unworthiness, shame etc.

Once we learn to recognise and identify negative thought patterns as they occur, we can start to step back from them. This process of stepping back from thoughts is called 'cognitive defusion.' In cognitive defusion we learn to see the thoughts in our head as simply thoughts and not reality.

When we can step back into cognitive defusion, we do not take our thoughts too seriously. We hold them lightly and only listen to them if we find them valuable or helpful.

As an example, imagine this: you wake up one day and look out the window and see that it's raining. A common thought some people might have is that the day is going to be bad because of the weather. Now, is it true that it's a bad day? No, it is simply raining. However, if you believe that thought (called 'cognitive fusion') you might actually end up thinking yourself into having a bad day. In other words, if you believe a negative thought, it can and will generate what we might call negativity.

It's completely normal to have negative thoughts. We all have minds that have evolved to be constantly on the lookout for problems and dangers, so most of us have minds prone to have many negative thoughts.

The problem arises when we believe our thoughts are true. When you are no longer entangled in thoughts they lose their grip on you and lose their power to generate unpleasant emotions.

It's important to be able to recognise the kinds of unhelpful thinking styles that can arise, so here are some other negative thinking patterns that are most common.

Anxious thoughts and worry: worry is when the mind projects into an imagined future and conjures up scenes and thoughts about what could go wrong. Here it often creates 'what if' scenarios.

Sometimes it takes the form of imagining or expecting that bad things will happen or that nothing good will ever happen for you. You might fret about your health deteriorating, your relationship going downhill, your car breaking down or your career being ruined—even though nothing has actually happened yet.

Criticism and self-beating: do you have a harsh inner critic? Are you always trying to whip yourself into shape, mentally beating yourself up for not being good enough yet? Are you on a perfection mission? Another pattern of negative thought is to constantly criticise and 'self improve' because you're not good enough yet. You may be very harsh on yourself, focusing in on all of your weaknesses and perceived flaws.

You may even extend this habit of criticism to others in your life. This can be the cause of tremendous strain on relationships. Negative self-talk and self-criticism often results in low self-esteem and a lack of confidence.

When the mind continuously hones in on what is wrong with yourself (and your life) and disassociates from what is going well and is good, we can become stuck in negativity.

Regret and guilt: ruminating on mistakes made in the past often creates feelings of shame, guilt and negativity. Feelings of worthlessness may arise when you play over and over in your mind, 'bad' choices or 'wrong' actions you feel you have made.

There is nothing negative about simply reflecting on past experiences. This is how we can learn, grow and mature as people. Negativity arises when you dwell on a situation repeatedly with no real intention to learn and grow, but instead you are self-beating or wishing things were different instead of being accepting of things as they are.

Problems: negative thoughts often revolve around what's wrong with your life. Your attention becomes fixated on, and exaggerates the so called negative aspects of your life. Here your mind will often downplay what is going well.

For example, you may have a wonderful family, food to eat and shelter, but your car breaks down and it's all you can think about and focus on all week long. You allow the situation with the car to dominate your thinking and negative emotions arise as a result.

Constantly focusing on that single problem is not constructive at all and is another way we can get trapped in negativity.

Key Two: Coming To Your Senses

Notice that many negative thoughts mostly flow from two directions. The first is dwelling on the past, the second is worrying about the future.

This may take the form of stress over whether or not you will achieve certain goals or anxiety about the security of your finances or relationships. Whatever your particular negative thoughts are, notice that in order to engage in negative thought patterns the mind needs to cast its focus mostly into past or future.

When lost in negative thinking, we tend to be so engrossed in thoughts that we completely lose touch with what is actually happening in the present moments of our lives. To become more present, and able to step out of negative thinking, one powerful method is to 'come to your senses'. To do this simply redirect your attention out of the thoughts in your head and bring your focus to your sense perceptions.

Whether you're in your home, at the office, in the park or on a subway, notice everything around you. Use your senses to their fullest. Don't get into a mental dialogue about the things you see, just be aware of what you're experiencing in this moment.

Research from Prof. Mark Williams from Oxford University showed that when difficulties arise in life, many of us tend to get caught up in excessive unhelpful thinking. Sometimes people try to stop constant unhelpful thinking, but we don't have to try to stop our thoughts. A more effective way to ease all that internal noise is to pay attention to our direct sensory experience. This way, there is little to no room left in our attention for all that excessive thinking. Coming to our senses calms the mind and grounds us in the present moment.

Key Three: Regular Mindfulness Practice

Mindfulness is the practice of waking up to that wellspring of wholeness and peace. It's waking up out of mind wandering (where we are lost in our heads, our old beliefs, habits, reactions and thinking patterns) so that we are able to live deliberately. Through mindfulness, we build our capacity to live from that deeper awareness and tame the mind.

Regular mindfulness meditation has been shown to decrease stress, depression and anxiety as well as improving immune function. People who practice meditation report overall levels of satisfaction with life higher than others. In fact, researcher and psychologist Matt Killingsworth found that what makes people most happy is being fully present in the moment and that the more our minds wander the more unhappy we become.

Four Ways You're Strengthening Your Mind When You Practice Meditation: each time your mind wanders in meditation, your task is to notice it and then detach from your thought stream and come back to your senses. This is a practice of untangling from thoughts over and over again, a habit which translates in the rest of your life too. It becomes a habit to notice and let go with ease.

Each time you let go of the thought stream and come back into the present moment, you tap into the stillness and wholeness at the heart of who you are. A sense of peace, lightness and joy arises more and more with each time you practice.

Key Four: Helpful questions For Unhelpful

Thoughts

Some kinds of negative thinking patterns can be quite 'sticky'. You may find that you try to 'name it to tame it' and come back to your senses, but the thoughts continue to have a grip on you. If you find yourself in this position, there are some further tools you can use to untangle from your thoughts and change your focus. These are called the 'Helpful questions for Unhelpful Thoughts'. These are drawn from ACT (Acceptance and Commitment Therapy).

Here are some questions you can ask yourself to help you untangle from negative thoughts.

• Is this thought in any way useful or helpful?

• Is it true? (Can I absolutely know that it's true?)

• Is this just an old story that my mind is playing out of habit?

• Does this thought help me take effective action?

• Is this though helpful or is my mind just babbling on?

• What do I really want to feel or create in the situation? How can I move towards that?

• How can I make the best of this situation?

• Who would I be without this negative thought?

• What new story or thought can I focus on now?

• How can I see this in a different or new way?

• What can I be grateful for in this moment?

Constructive thinking allows you to be happy when things are going good, and puts problems in perspective when times get tough so you can stay calm and clear headed and deal with them in a practical and efficient way.

Practicing The Four Keys

The four keys are not a quick fix method for creating permanent change of long standing patterns. You will find that in any given moment of negativity, these tools will be of great help in assisting you and change your way of thinking and your mindset. The more you practice these tools, the more they will become like second nature to you. It is essentially like building a muscle.

How to Improve Your Mental Health

Mental health is much more than a diagnosis. It's your overall psychological well-being—the way you feel about yourself and others as well as your ability to manage your feelings and deal with everyday difficulties. And while taking care of your mental health can mean seeking professional support and treatment, it also means taking steps to improve your emotional health on your own. Making these changes will pay off in all aspects of your life. It can boost your mood, build resilience, and add to your overall enjoyment of life.

Tell yourself something positive: research shows that how you think about yourself can have a powerful effect on how you feel. When we perceive our selves and our life negatively, we can end up viewing experiences in a way that confirms that notion. Instead, practice using words that promote feelings of self-worth and personal power. For example, instead of saying, "I'm such a loser. I won't get the job because I tanked in the interview," try, "I didn't do as well in the interview as I would have liked, but that doesn't mean I'm not going to get the job."

Write down something you are grateful for: gratitude has been clearly linked with improved well-being and mental health, as well as happiness. The best-researched method to increase feelings of gratitude is to keep a gratitude journal or write a daily gratitude list. Generally contemplating gratitude is also effective, but you need to get regular practice to experience long-term benefit. Find something to be grateful for, let it fill your heart, and bask in that feeling.

Focus on one thing (in the moment): being mindful of the present moment allows us to let go of negative or difficult emotions from past experiences that weigh us down. Start by bringing awareness to routine activities, such as taking a shower, eating lunch, or walking home. Paying attention to the physical sensations, sounds, smells, or tastes of these experiences helps you focus. When your mind wanders, just bring it back to what you are doing.

Exercise: your body releases stress-relieving and mood-boosting endorphins before and after you work out, which is why exercise is a powerful antidote to stress, anxiety, and depression. Look for small ways to add activity to your day, like taking the stairs instead of the elevator or going on a short walk. To get the most benefit, aim for at least 30 minutes of exercise daily, and try to do it outdoors. Exposure to sunlight helps your body produce vitamin D, which increases your level of serotonin in the brain.

Eat a good meal: what you eat nourishes your whole body, including your brain. Carbohydrates (in moderate amounts) increase serotonin, a chemical that has been shown to have a calming effect on your mood. Protein-rich foods increase norepinephrine, dopamine, and tyrosine, which help keep you alert. Vegetables and fruits are loaded with nutrients that feed every cell of your body, including those that affect mood-regulating brain chemicals. Include foods with Omega-3 polyunsaturated fatty acids (found in fish, nuts, and flaxseed.) Research shows that these nutrients can improve mood and restore structural integrity to the brain cells necessary for cognitive function.

Open up to someone: knowing you are valued by others is important for helping you think more positively. Plus, being more trusting can increase your emotional well-being because, as you get better at finding the positive aspects in other people, you become better at recognizing your own.

Do something for someone else: being helpful to others has a beneficial effect on how you feel about yourself. Being helpful and kind, and valued for what you do, is a great way to build self-esteem. The meaning you find in helping others will enrich and expand your life.

Take a break: in those moments when it all seems like too much, step away until you feel a little better. Sometimes, the best thing to do is a simple breathing exercise: close your eyes and take 10 deep breaths. For each one, count to four as you inhale, hold it for a count of four, and then exhale for another four.

Go to bed on time: sleep deprivation has a significant negative effect on your mood. Try to go to bed at a regular time each day, and practice good habits to get better sleep. These include shutting down screens for at least an hour before bed, using your bed only for sleep or relaxing activities, and restricting caffeinated drinks for the morning.

You have the power to take positive steps right now to improve your resilience and emotional health. Don't wait until you're in a crisis to make your mental health a priority. Pick something from this section that resonates with you and try it. Then, try something else. Slowly putting in place routines, habits, and regular patterns will help you feel better through gradual change.

APPLYING BEHAVIORAL TECHNIQUES

You and your therapist can mix and match techniques depending on what you're most interested in trying and what works for you. You can also try the following Cognitive Behavioral Therapy techniques as self-help.

Pleasant Activity Scheduling

Pleasant activity scheduling is a surprisingly effective Cognitive Behavioral Therapy technique. It's particularly helpful for depression.

Try this: write the next seven days down on a piece of paper, starting with today. For each day, schedule one pleasant activity (anything you enjoy that is not unhealthy) that you wouldn't normally do. It could be as simple as reading a chapter of a novel or eating your lunch away from your desk without rushing.

An alternative version of this technique is to also schedule an activity a day that gives you a sense of mastery, competence, or accomplishment. Again, choose something small that you wouldn't usually do. Aim for something that will take you less than ten minutes.

An advanced version of this technique would be to schedule three pleasant activities per day - one for sometime during your morning, one for the afternoon, and one for evening.

Doing activities that produce higher levels of positive emotions in your daily life will help make your thinking less negative, narrow, rigid, and self-focused.

Situation Exposure Hierarchies

Situation exposure hierarchies involve putting things you would normally avoid on a list. For example, a client with an eating disorder might make a list of forbidden foods, with ice cream at the top of the list and full fat yogurt near the bottom. A client with social anxiety might put asking someone on a date at the top of her list and asking a woman for directions near the bottom of her list. For each item on your list, rate how distressed you think you'd be if you did it. Use a scale from 0-10. For example, ice-cream = 10, full fat yogurt = 2. Order your list from highest to lowest. The theme of the list should reflect your problem.

Try to have several items at each distress number so there are no big jumps. The idea is to work your way through the list from lowest to highest. You would likely experiment with each item several times over a period of a few days until the distress you feel about being in that situation is about half of what it was the first time you tried it (e.g., you can eat full fat yogurt with only 1/10 distress instead of 2/10). Then move to the next item up the list.

Imagery Based Exposure

One version of imagery exposure involves bringing to mind a recent memory that provoked strong negative emotions. Imagery based exposure can help counteract rumination because it helps make intrusive painful memories less likely to trigger overthinking mechanisms. Because of this, it also tends to help reduce avoidance coping. When a person is less distressed by intrusive memories, they're able to choose healthier coping actions.

Cognitive Rehearsal

In this technique, the patient is asked to recall a problematic situation from his/her past. The therapist and patient work on the problem to find a solution for it. The therapist asks the patient to rehearse positive thoughts in his/her mind; rehearsing positive thoughts helps in making appropriate changes to the patient's thought processes. The power of imagination proves to be of great help when you are doing such type of exercises.

Validity Testing

Validity of thoughts of the patient are tested by the therapist; the patient is allowed to defend his/her viewpoint with the help of an objective evidence. The faulty nature or invalidity of beliefs held by the patient is exposed if he/she is unable to produce any kind of objective evidence.

Guided Discovery

The purpose behind using this technique is to help patients understand their cognitive distortions. Patients are offered the necessary assistance and guidance by therapists to understand how they process information. It allows patients to alter the way they process of information. Upon completion of this treatment, the patient's perception of the world undergoes a profound change and he/she starts seeing things with a new outlook. A change in perception enables the patient to modify his/her behavioral patterns.

Modeling

This is one of the important cognitive behavioral therapy techniques wherein therapists perform role-playing exercises. These cognitive behavioral therapy exercises teach patients how to respond in difficult situations. The patient sees the behavior of the therapist as a model to overcome his/her own behavioral problems.

Homework

'Homework' is actually a set of assignments to be completed by patients. During their sessions with therapists, the patients are asked to take down notes, review audiotapes of these sessions and read books related to this therapy.

Aversive Conditioning

In this technique, the appeal of maladaptive behavior is lessened with the help of 'dissuasion'. The patient is exposed to an unpleasant stimulus while he/she is engaged in a particular behavior for which treatment is needed. The end result of this exercise is that the patient learns to associates the unpleasant stimulus with the maladaptive behavior in question; he/she becomes averse to behaving in such a manner.

Systematic Positive Reinforcement

A technique in which a certain kind of behavior (positive) is rewarded with positive reinforcement. A reward system is used to reinforce the importance of positive behavior in the minds of patients.

Cognitive Behavioral Therapy for Depression

CBT is one of the effective therapies used for treating mild depression. This therapy is considered to be as effective as treatment with antidepressant medication. CBT is known to deliver good results in adults as well as adolescents. This kind of treatment can be most effective when the patient is motivated enough to overcome his/her behavioral problems.

CBT for Children

Cognitive behavioral therapy for children requires the therapist to play an active role in the treatment. This is because children are not capable of labeling or describing their thoughts and feelings as accurately as adults do. Therefore, the therapist has to perform the crucial job of extracting necessary information about the child's thoughts and behavioral patterns. It is also important that CBT sessions for children are completed in a short span of time.

Structured Format of CBT

The structured model of CBT makes this therapy more effective than most other psychotherapy techniques. CBT is basically a time-bound therapy during which the client (patient) has to attend sessions with a therapist. The patient has to do some homework before attending the next; which means, he/she is required to actively participating in the whole process.

The cognitive behavioral therapy techniques help in solving many problems that occur from maladaptive thoughts and behavioral patterns. Therapists and patients (clients) make use of the above-mentioned techniques to cure most of the psychological problems in a time-bound and effective manner.

LEARNING TO ANCHOR
THE POSITIVE CHANGES

For most people procrastination, irrespective of what they say, is NOT about being lazy. In fact, when we procrastinate we often work intensely for long stretches of time just before our deadlines. Working long and hard is the opposite of lazy, so that can't be the reason we do it. So, why do we procrastinate? And, more importantly, what can we do about it?

As suggested above, some say they procrastinate because they are lazy. Others claim they "do better" when they procrastinate and "work best" under pressure.

Virtually everyone who says this habitually procrastinates and has not completed an important academic task in which they made a plan, implemented it, had time to review, etc. before their deadline. So, in reality, they can't make a comparison about the circumstances they work best under. If you always procrastinate and never really approach your tasks systematically, then you can't accurately say that you know you "do better" under pressure. Still, other people say they like the "rush" of leaving things to the end and meeting a deadline

Procrastination is not a matter of solely having poor

time management skills, but rather can be traced to underlying and more complex psychological reasons. These dynamics are often made worse by schools where students are constantly being evaluated, and especially in college where the pressure for grades is high and a lot can be riding on students' performance. In reality, procrastination is often a self-protection strategy for students. For example, if you procrastinate, then you always have the excuse of "not having enough" time in the event that you fail, so your sense of your ability is never threatened. When there is so much pressure on getting a good grade, it's no wonder that students want to avoid it and put off their work. For the most part, our reasons for delaying and avoiding are rooted in fear and anxiety-about doing poorly. We avoid doing work to avoid our abilities being judged. And, if we happen to succeed, we feel that much "smarter." So, what can we do to overcome our tendencies to procrastinate?

Awareness: The First Step

To overcome procrastination you need to have an understanding of the reasons why you procrastinate and the function procrastination serves in your life. You can't come up with an effective solution if you don't really understand the root of the problem. As with most problems, awareness and self-knowledge are the keys to figuring out how to stop procrastinating.

Time Management Techniques: One Piece of the

Puzzle

To overcome procrastination, time management techniques and tools are indispensable, but they are not enough by themselves. Not all methods of managing time are equally helpful in dealing with procrastination. For instance, making a huge list of things to do or scheduling every minute of your day may increase your stress and thus procrastination. Instead, set reasonable goals (e.g. a manageable list of things to do), break big tasks down, and give yourself flexibility and allot time to do things you enjoy as rewards for the work you have completed.

Motivation: Finding Productive Reasons for Engaging in Tasks

To overcome procrastination, it's critical that you stay motivated in order to be productive. A good way to put positive motives in motion is to set and focus on your goals. Identify and write down your own personal reasons for enrolling in a course and monitor your progress toward your goals using a goal-setting chart. Remember to focus on your reasons and your goals.

Staying Motivated: Be Active to be Engaged

Another key to overcoming procrastination is to stay actively engaged in your classes. If you are passive in class you're probably not understanding the course and its topics, and that weakens your motivation. If you are passive, you are probably not making as much sense out of the course and course materials as you could. Nonsense and confusion are not engaging; in fact, they are boring and frustrating. Prevent that by aiming to really understand course material. Try seeking out what is interesting and relevant to you in the course materials, setting your own purpose for every reading and class session, and asking yourself (and others) questions about what you are learning.

Summary of Tips for Overcoming Procrastination

Awareness: reflect on the reasons why you procrastinate, your habits and thoughts that lead to procrastinating.

Assess: what feelings lead to procrastinating, and how does it make you feel? Are these positive, productive feelings? Do you want to change them?

Outlook: alter your perspective. Looking at a big task in terms of smaller pieces makes it less intimidating. Look for what's appealing about, or what you want to get out of, an assignment (beyond just the grade).

Commit: if you feel stuck, start simply by committing to complete a small task, any task, and write it down. Finish it and reward yourself. Write down on your schedule or to do list only what you can completely commit to, and if you write it down, follow through no matter what. By doing so, you will slowly rebuild trust in yourself that you will really do what you say you will, which so many procrastinators have lost.

Surroundings: when doing school work, choose wisely where and with whom you are working. Repeatedly placing yourself in situations where you don't get much done, such as studying in your bed, at a cafe or with friends, can actually be a method of avoiding work.

Goals: focus on what you want to do, not what you want to avoid. Think about the productive reasons for doing a task by setting positive, concrete, meaningful learning and achievement goals for yourself.

Be realistic: achieving goals and changing habits takes time and effort; don't sabotage yourself by having unrealistic expectations that you cannot meet.

Self-talk: notice how you are thinking, and talking to yourself. Talk to yourself in ways that remind you of your goals and replace old, counter-productive habits of self-talk. Instead of saying, "I wish I hadn't... " say, "I will ..."

Un-schedule: if you feel stuck, you probably won't use a schedule that is a constant reminder of all that you have to do and is all work and no play. So, make a largely unstructured, flexible schedule in which you slot in only what is necessary. Keep track of any time you spend working toward your goals and reward yourself for it. This can reduce feelings of being overwhelmed and increase satisfaction in what you get done.

Swiss Cheese It: breaking down big tasks into little ones is a good approach. A variation on this is devoting short chunks of time to a big task and doing as much as you can in that time with few expectations about what you will get done. For example, try spending about ten minutes just jotting down ideas that come to mind on the topic of a paper, or skimming over a long reading to get just the main ideas. After doing this several times on a big task, you will have made some progress on it, you'll have some momentum, you'll have less work to do to complete the task, and it won't seem so huge because you've punched holes in it (like Swiss cheese). In short, it'll be easier to complete the task because you've gotten started and removed some of the obstacles to finishing.

HOW TO OVERCOME NEGATIVE BELIEFS

People's emotional reactions and behaviour are strongly influenced by core beliefs. Core beliefs are essential part of the individual's cognition. Cognition comprises thoughts, beliefs and interpretations about the self or the situations. In other words, one's cognition is the meaning one gives to the events of his/her life.

Different cognitions generate different emotions

If we ask people what has made them sad (or happy, or angry) they often give us accounts of events or situations. If an event automatically gave rise to an emotion in such a straightforward way, then it would follow that the same event would have to result in the same emotion for anyone who experienced that event. What we see actually is that to a greater or lesser degree, people react differently to similar events. Even events such as suffering bereavement, or being diagnosed with an inoperable stage of cancer, which are obviously terrible, do not produce the same emotional state in everyone. Some may completely be crushed by such events, while others cope reasonably well. When two people react differently to an event it is because they are seeing it differently.

Different levels of cognitive processes

Cognition has different levels. Some cognitive processes are in the consciousness and we are aware of them. Negative thinking and negative thoughts automatically generated when an incident occurs are in the uppermost level.

Core beliefs

Core beliefs represent the bottom line of a person's mind. These are the fundamental beliefs about oneself, other people and the world in general. Characteristics of core beliefs are:

1. They are not immediately accessible to consciousness. They may have to be inferred by observation of one's characteristic thoughts and behaviours in many different situations.

2. They manifest as general and absolute statements. (E. g. I am bad. Others are not to be trusted.)

3. Unlike negative automatic thoughts, core belief do not vary much across times or situations, but are seen by the person as fundamental truths that apply in all situations.

4. They are usually learned early in life as a result of childhood experiences, but they may sometimes develop or change later in life, e.g., as a result of severe traumatic experience.

Change your core beliefs to avoid stress and prevent psychological disorders

Psychological disorders like generalized anxiety disorder, panic disorder, depression, phobias, and obsessive compulsive disorder spring from the negative core beliefs. Changing negative core beliefs helps the individual to deal with their psychological disorders. The first step in changing a core belief is to identify it. When you do a thorough job of identifying the core beliefs, you are more than halfway to changing them. This task can be a little challenging in the beginning, but gets easier with practice.

How to identify the core belief?

Identifying a core belief is like solving a mystery of the illusions in your mind. You have to follow some clues to get down to the hidden beliefs in the unconscious. Let's use the example of fear of public speaking. Fear of public speaking is an emotional reaction to a belief. The underlying thought a person has is that, "They will think I'm stupid." This is the fear, but not the belief. Fears associated with what other people think of us are very common. This same thought can occur in the mind when asking for what we want.

However the thought is not a core belief. One has to be careful here because they are often misleading. When finding core beliefs you follow the emotion. We have to keep asking how the emotion of fear is created by the act of what someone else thinks.

If someone pointed at your hair, claimed it was green, and then started to laugh out loud at how silly you looked would you feel hurt? Probably not. You know the issue is with their perception and not with you. Having someone make fun of you and laugh at you when you know it is their perception is not a problem for you. What people think of you doesn't hurt you at all.

When you don't believe you look foolish you are not affected by what others think. Being aware that their mental image of you is not actual you, gives you immunity to their opinion. With this understanding, it is obvious that one cannot be hurt emotionally by what others think and say about him/her.

Steps to Changing Core Beliefs

When you fully identify a set of beliefs, you instinctively divest your belief in them. This shift happens just through your expanded awareness. Just by identifying your beliefs, you facilitate change in your emotions and behavior without a lot of work.

Changing a core belief is surprisingly easy. You simply stop believing in them. It doesn't take much effort to not believe something. However, it does take some effort to develop the awareness to identify them.

It sounds simple, but does require some work. There is

also one very important step in the process that is often missed. You have to change your point of view in order to change a core belief. Where you shift your point of view in your mind is critically important. Certain points of view will make it easy to dissolve a core belief and others will stop the process.

Changing Core Beliefs by Shifting Point of View

An easier way to change a belief is through shifting point of view. A new perspective allows you to have awareness that changes the way you see things.

Without this shift in perspective, it is very difficult to change a belief. When you are within the paradigm of a false belief, it appears completely true thus you continue to believe in it.

A belief paradigm acts very much like a dream when you are asleep. When you are in a dream, it seems completely real. You believe what is happening in the dream is really happening to you. You might feel like your life is in danger and feel the corresponding emotions of fear, but when you wake up from the dream, you begin looking at it from the perspective of sitting up in your bed in an awakened state. With that shift in point of view, you immediately drop your fear and the notion that you are in danger. Changing your point of view in this way allows you to quickly change beliefs. This kind of paradigm shift is very powerful. Numerous people have had near death experiences that completely dissolved their fears of death and dying. Real life change involves changing core beliefs. One of the fastest ways to change core beliefs is by shifting your point of view.

Keeping a thought diary helps to identify negative core beliefs

Following this guideline for writing a thought diary:

1. *The situation:* briefly describe the situation you would like to have handled better. This will help you remember it later if you want to review your notes.

2. *Initial thought:* what thought first popped into your mind? This was probably a subconscious or automatic thought that you have had before.

3. *Negative thinking:* identify the negative thinking behind your initial thought. Choose one or more from the list of common types of negative thinking.

4. *Source of negative belief:* can you trace your thinking back to a situation or person? Is there a deep belief or fear driving your thinking?

5. *Challenge your thinking:* look at the evidence both for and against your thinking. Have you been in a similar situation before? What did you learn from it? What strengths do you bring to this situation? Make sure you see the whole picture.

6. *Consider the consequences:* what are the short-term

and long-term consequences if you continue to think like this? Look at the physical, psychological, professional, and emotional consequences.

7. *Alternative thinking:* the previous steps of the thought record helped you understand your thinking and lower your defenses. Now that you've considered the facts, write down a healthier way of thinking.

8. *Positive belief and affirmation:* write down a statement that reflects your healthier beliefs. Find something that you can repeat to yourself.

9. *Action plan:* what action can you take to support your new thinking?

10. *Improvement:* do you feel slightly better or more optimistic? This step reinforces the idea that if you change your thinking, you will change your mood. Gradually, your thinking and life will begin to improve.

If you write a thought record every day for a few weeks, you will begin to change your thinking. You'll spot your negative thinking quickly and let it go. You will come up with better alternatives. You will practice your healthier way of thinking and incorporate it into your life.

A Negative Thought as a Flame

Visualize a negative thought as a flame. A flame burning in an empty concrete parking lot cannot do much damage. These fires are left to burn out on its own or easily extinguished.

Put that flame in a closed room filled with combustible material, and you have a potential disaster on your hands.

Unless quickly extinguished, the fire will use every piece of flammable material in that room to burn hotter, longer and faster. Left uninterrupted, that single flame will become an inextinguishable inferno that will burn until it has nothing left to fuel its flames.

People experience a similar situation when they are a host for so much negativity. By the time it finally runs its course, all the anger, frustration, and blame has destroyed a person from mental, physical and spiritual exhaustion.

Recognizing the triggers

In order to avoid a negative spin, you need to recognize the triggers that set off the cycle and the environments that make you more susceptible to these triggers.

Being in a positive state of mind or in a secure and nurturing environment allows for a measure of protection from a negative cycle.

Add another layer of defence by being mindful of your work environment, the type of career you choose and the interactions you have with people.

Weakening Triggers

Create an inventory of positive truths about yourself

and your life. It takes a little bit of effort to remember the positive aspects of your life, but it is well worth the work.

Disarming triggers requires that you counter any negative thought with a relevant and equally powerful positive truth.

For example, if you think "Everyone hates me, I'm unlovable", you can counteract this thought by thinking, "My wife and children love me and they are always happy to see me when I come home." Extinguish the negative thought as quickly as it arises.

Be truthful and celebrate the good in your life. Take five minutes every night to write down all your successes, positive qualities and the things that make you happy. This creates a natural defence against negativity.

Disrupting the cycle by disrupting the pattern

There are going to be times when you are unable to recognize a trigger because you are in a weak mental state.

For example, you go to sleep in a positive state of mind and then unexpectedly wake up angry and grumpy. In these scenarios, breaking a negative cycle with positive thoughts is hard, if not impossible, to do.

In cases like this, starve yourself of any additional negative energy that might strengthen your state of mind. This requires you to break any established patterns.

If the usual routine includes having a coffee and reading a newspaper, then you have to catch your mind off guard and go straight to the shower.

FEAR IN THE BRAIN

Fear may be as old as life on Earth. It is a fundamental, deeply wired reaction, evolved over the history of biology, to protect organisms against perceived threat to their integrity or existence. Fear may be as simple as a cringe of an antenna in a snail that is touched, or as complex as existential anxiety in a human.

Whether we love or hate to experience fear, it's hard to deny that we certainly revere it – devoting an entire holiday to the celebration of fear.

Thinking about the circuitry of the brain and human psychology, some of the main chemicals that contribute to the "fight or flight" response are also involved in other positive emotional states, such as happiness and excitement. So, it makes sense that the high arousal state we experience during a scare may also be experienced in a more positive light. But what makes the difference between getting a "rush" and feeling completely terrorized?

We are psychiatrists who treat fear and study its neurobiology. Our studies and clinical interactions, as well as those of others, suggest that a major factor in how we experience fear has to do with the context. When our "thinking" brain gives feedback to our "emotional" brain and we perceive ourselves as being in a safe space, we can then quickly shift the way we experience that high arousal state, going from one of fear to one of enjoyment or excitement.

When you enter a haunted house during Halloween season, for example, anticipating a ghoul jumping out at you and knowing it isn't really a threat, you are able to quickly relabel the experience. In contrast, if you were walking in a dark alley at night and a stranger began chasing you, both your emotional and thinking areas of the brain would be in agreement that the situation is dangerous, and it's time to flee!

But how does your brain do this?

Fear reaction starts in the brain and spreads through the body to make adjustments for the best defense, or flight reaction. The fear response starts in a region of the brain called the amygdala. This almond-shaped set of nuclei in the temporal lobe of the brain is dedicated to detecting the emotional salience of the stimuli – how much something stands out to us.

For example, the amygdala activates whenever we see a human face with an emotion. This reaction is more pronounced with anger and fear. A threat stimulus, such as the sight of a predator, triggers a fear response in the amygdala, which activates areas involved in preparation for motor functions involved in fight or flight. It also triggers release of stress hormones and sympathetic nervous system.

This leads to bodily changes that prepare us to be more

efficient in a danger: The brain becomes hyperalert, pupils dilate, the bronchi dilate and breathing accelerates. Heart rate and blood pressure rise. Blood flow and stream of glucose to the skeletal muscles increase. Organs not vital in survival such as the gastrointestinal system slow down.

A part of the brain called the hippocampus is closely connected with the amygdala. The hippocampus and prefrontal cortex help the brain interpret the perceived threat. They are involved in a higher-level processing of context, which helps a person know whether a perceived threat is real.

For instance, seeing a lion in the wild can trigger a strong fear reaction, but the response to a view of the same lion at a zoo is more of curiosity and thinking that the lion is cute. This is because the hippocampus and the frontal cortex process contextual information, and inhibitory pathways dampen the amygdala fear response and its downstream results. Basically, our "thinking" circuitry of brain reassures our "emotional" areas that we are, in fact, OK.

Similar to other animals, we very often learn fear through personal experiences, such as being attacked by an aggressive dog, or observing other humans being attacked by an aggressive dog.

However, an evolutionarily unique and fascinating way of learning in humans is through instruction – we learn from the spoken words or written notes! If a sign says the dog is dangerous, proximity to the dog will trigger a fear response.

We learn safety in a similar fashion: experiencing a domesticated dog, observing other people safely interact with that dog or reading a sign that the dog is friendly.

Fear creates distraction, which can be a positive experience. When something scary happens, in that moment, we are on high alert and not preoccupied with other things that might be on our mind (getting in trouble at work, worrying about a big test the next day), which brings us to the here and now.

Furthermore, when we experience these frightening things with the people in our lives, we often find that emotions can be contagious in a positive way. We are social creatures, able to learn from one another. So, when you look over to your friend at the haunted house and she's quickly gone from screaming to laughing, socially you're able to pick up on her emotional state, which can positively influence your own.

While each of these factors - context, distraction, social learning - have potential to influence the way we experience fear, a common theme that connects all of them is our sense of control. When we are able to recognize what is and isn't a real threat, relabel an experience and enjoy the thrill of that moment, we are ultimately at a place where we feel in control. That perception of control is vital to how we experience and respond to fear. When we overcome the initial "fight or flight" rush, we are often left feeling satisfied, reassured of our safety and more confident in our ability to confront the things that initially scared us.

It is important to keep in mind that everyone is different, with a unique sense of what we find scary or enjoyable. This raises yet another question: While many can enjoy a good fright, why might others downright hate it?

Any imbalance between excitement caused by fear in the animal brain and the sense of control in the contextual human brain may cause too much, or not enough, excitement. If the individual perceives the experience as "too real," an extreme fear response can overcome the sense of control over the situation.

This may happen even in those who do love scary experiences: They may enjoy Freddy Krueger movies but be too terrified by "The Exorcist," as it feels too real, and fear response is not modulated by the cortical brain.

On the other hand, if the experience is not triggering enough to the emotional brain, or if is too unreal to the thinking cognitive brain, the experience can end up feeling boring. A biologist who cannot tune down her cognitive brain from analyzing all the bodily things that are realistically impossible in a zombie movie may not be able to enjoy "The Walking Dead" as much as another person.

So if the emotional brain is too terrified and the cognitive brain helpless, or if the emotional brain is bored and the cognitive brain is too suppressing, scary movies and experiences may not be as fun.

All fun aside, abnormal levels of fear and anxiety can lead to significant distress and dysfunction and limit a person's ability for success and joy of life. Nearly one in four people experiences a form of anxiety disorder during their lives, and nearly 8 percent experience post-traumatic stress disorder (PTSD).

Disorders of anxiety and fear include phobias, social phobia, generalized anxiety disorder, separation anxiety, PTSD and obsessive compulsive disorder. These conditions usually begin at a young age, and without appropriate treatment can become chronic and debilitating and affect a person's life trajectory. The good news is that we have effective treatments that work in a relatively short time period, in the form of psychotherapy and medications.

Surefire ways to get rid of bad habits

Success, happiness and good health often elude us not because we lack good habits but because we have bad habits. Sometimes they are habits like procrastination or mindless spending. But at other times they can be addictions like smoking and gambling.

Knowing how our bad habits negatively influence our lives is rarely enough to break them. For example, all smokers are aware of the health consequences of smoking. Diseased lungs are displayed prominently in every cigarette pack. There would be no smokers in the world today if that worked.

This fails to work because we don't do our bad habits for the reasons we should not do them. No smoker has ever smoked a cigarette to get cancer. Students don't procrastinate to fail. So in order to break our bad habits, we must first remove the reason why we do them. In other words, we need to eliminate the desire to do the habit.

Once the desire is gone, it takes no willpower to break bad habits, just as it doesn't take willpower to not do things we have no desire to do. It doesn't take much effort to stop yourself from eating live frogs because you have no desire to do it. Breaking your bad habits can be just as effortless. You just need the right belief and the right system.

Our Habits Controls Us

From the outside, it would seem that our bad habits is a matter of choice. Smokers, for example, do make the choice of trying their first cigarette. But no smoker has ever made a decision that they will keep smoking for the rest of their lives. We often fall into the trap thinking we can stop whenever we want, only to realize that we no longer have any control. When we watch the first episode of a TV show, we end up binge watching multiple seasons at a stretch because we cannot stop ourselves. Every addict wishes inside that he had never started because life was fine before their addiction but now they are hooked and cannot enjoy life without satisfying their craving.

Researchers from National Institute on Alcohol Abuse and Alcoholism trained rats to press a lever to get a piece food. The researchers later electrified the floor so that when the rat walked to get the food, it received a shock. In a different experimental setting, the rat recognized the danger in the electric floor and would avoid it. But when the rat saw the lever, the habits took over and the rat would press the lever and go for the food and get electrocuted every time. The rat could not stop itself in spite of being aware of the danger because the habits were so strong.

Similarly, dieters find it hard to resist junk, smokers struggle to quit and students procrastinate on their assignments in spite of being aware of the consequences it has on their lives. Strong habits create an obsessive craving which makes our brain behave on autopilot even if there are strong disincentives like loss of job, health, reputation, family or home.

When We Use Willpower to quit, We Fail

We usually try to break bad habits using willpower, which makes us feel we are making a sacrifice. A Harvard study showed the 12 month success rates of people who used the willpower method to quit smoking with no education or support was 6%.

When using willpower to quit, we find life extremely unpleasant and difficult and have to be cautious all the time to prevent relapse. This is because the desire to do the habit always remains inside us.

10 % of former smokers who abstained from smoking for ten years showed ongoing cravings even years later. Mere abstinence does not mean we have broken our habit. It just means we don't allow ourselves to do our habit. A person who does not drink alcohol but who is constantly thinking about alcohol is not a non-alcoholic but is an alcoholic who does not let himself drink.

We see the benefits of breaking our habits but also believe it provides us with something which we are now depriving ourselves of. This makes us miserable, vulnerable and increases desire that begins to obsess us. We try to overcome this by not thinking about our craving but that only makes us more obsessed.

Believing our problems can be easily solved by doing our bad habits we begin to question our decision to break our bad habits. Finally, we accept defeat and cave in. This minor relapse makes us feel bad and we indulge in the very same habit that made us feel bad, to feel better.

We fail to break our bad habits not because we lack willpower but because we don't eliminate desire. Without desire, willpower is not required to stop, just as it doesn't take willpower to not do the things we have no desire to do.

Why Does Our Brain Form Habits If They Are Bad?

Habits is a way for the brain to save effort by making rewarding behaviour automatic. Without habits, you will have to relearn how to brush your teeth every morning. Habits are useful but the problem is our brain cannot tell the difference between good and bad habits. Behavior that gives us short-term rewards often becomes habits, even if they cause long-term harm. Overeating, procrastinating and smoking becomes habit easily because the rewards are instant and the pain comes later. Developing the habit of exercising is harder because the reward comes later.

Schultz from the University of Cambridge, trained a monkey named Julio to pull a lever when a shape appeared on computer screen. Pulling the lever gave Julio a drop of blackberry juice which made the pleasure centres of his brain light up. When his brain started craving for the juice, Julio was glued to the monitor like a gambler in a slot machine. If the juice arrived late or diluted, this craving would turn into anger

& depression.

Charles Duhigg's book, "The Power of Habit" focuses on the 3 components of a habit. The first component is the trigger, which tells the brain to start doing a particular behaviour (shapes in Julio's monitor). The second component is the behaviour that is done (Julio pulling the lever). The third part is the reward for doing the behaviour (Julio's blackberry juice). The habit is formed when the brain starts to crave for the reward as soon as the brain sees the trigger. There is nothing programmed in our brains that makes us want to overeat or smoke. But over time we slowly develop a neurological craving for these things.

Break The Habit By Seeing The Reward As An Illusion

The first step to breaking your bad habit is identifying the reward.

What do you really get doing your habit?

If the rewards you think your habits provided were actually real, then you can break your bad habits, simply by switching your existing habit with a healthier behavior that provided the same reward. For example, if you eat junk at work for distraction, then you can break your habit simply by replacing eating junk with a healthier distraction that does not add to your waistline. This is the premise of the book "The Power of Habit" and this works well for weaker habits. But try telling a smoker to resist his urge for smoking when he is bored by entertaining himself on YouTube. He won't be a successful non-smoker for very long. This is because most rewards of our habits are illusions.

We often rationalize why we do our bad habits but all the reasons we use to justify our behaviour are an illusion, excuses, fallacies or based on myth. For example, smokers believe they need cigarettes to relax, relieve stress, to concentrate or to relieve boredom. But cigarettes do not give them any of this. If it did, they should be a lot more relaxed, focused and less bored than non-smokers.

Most of us brainwash ourselves in a certain way that keeps us doing our bad habits. Only by identifying what we think is the reward can we address and remove the myths we have about the reward. When we begin to see through the illusory rewards, we eliminate desire by realizing that there is nothing to give up.

What We Give Up When We Break Bad Habits?

What are we giving up when we break our bad habits? Well, most of the time you are giving up absolutely nothing.

We don't do our bad habits for pleasure. We do it to feel normal. This feels like pleasure. A drug addict feels miserable, anxious, stressed and angry when he is deprived of his drug. When he shoots up his drug, he gets relief from all the negative symptoms. The subsequent dose partially relieves the symptoms but also ensures that the addict goes through withdrawal again. This keeps the addict stuck in the vicious habit loop. Normal people do not experience the symptoms of the drug addict. When we look at this it is obvious to us that the symptoms the drug addict experiences are caused by the drug, not removed by it. But we fail to have the same understanding when it comes to our bad habits.

Our bad habits cause symptoms of craving that normal people don't experience. We do our bad habits to partially relieve the symptoms but it only keeps us stuck in the vicious habit loop ensuring we experience the symptoms of craving again.

Unlike drug addiction which might require a visit to rehab, the craving caused by most bad habits including alcohol and smoking can be killed immediately when the belief system is changed. If you are not entirely convinced that there is nothing to give up, you need to examine the rewards of your bad habits and see them for what they really are. Otherwise, you will feel craving and will have to use willpower to prevent relapse.

The 4 Illusory Rewards

If you think your habit provides any of the following 4 rewards, you probably have an illusory reward:

1. Relieves stress

2. Relieves boredom

3. Improves concentration

4. Relieves anxiety and gives confidence

We will address the common myths people have about each of these rewards which will help dispel the illusion.

Reward 1 - Relief From Stress & Relaxation

For many, habits provide relaxation and relief from stress. We all have several things stressing us out. Not just big tragedies but relatively minor things like work deadlines. We do our bad habits to relieve this stress and the stress does seem to go away. But what has really happened?

Apart from the environmental stress, we experience additional stress because of the aggravation caused by craving. Bad habits relieve this portion of stress it created through craving. But our real-world stress like work deadlines continues to exist. When we do our habits we feel better able to cope with this stress because we temporarily don't have the additional stress caused by the craving to deal with.

A study has shown that we fall back into our habits when we are stressed because we feel less anxiety and more in control when we do our habits. People who have been sober for years relapse when a major life catastrophe happens like a death of a loved one or divorce. This is because of a failure to understand that alcohol does not relieve stress but only adds to the problem.

The habits that we fall back on during times of stress need not be bad. In a study, students who habitually ate a healthy breakfast continued to eat healthy during the stressful period of their exams. Whereas students who gained extra weight during their exams had a habit of eating unhealthy. Consciously engineering your habits is important so that your habits make you better and not worse during times of stress.

Reward 2 - Relief From Boredom

Some people do their habit because they are bored. Boredom is a frame of mind and not a physical condition that can be cured. Initially, we are bored. Now we are bored and engaged in self-destructive behaviour. Our bad habits do not cure boredom. It just creates a temporary distraction that allows us to forget that we are bored.

If our bad habits did relieve boredom, then why do we have to engage in it multiple times or do it for longer periods at a stretch?

Most bad habits rob us of our energy and make us more lethargic, putting us in a state of mind where we cannot do anything else. Instead of doing something when bored like how a normal person would, we lounge around, do our bad habit and feel more bored.

If you know someone who plays excessive video games or who spends hours in front of the TV, you will see they are not any less bored. They will be extremely tired and will feel like shit for wasting so much time.

Reward 3 - Helps Concentration & Removes Mental Block

If you think your bad habits removes mental blocks and improves concentration, then you are not alone. Some of the greatest artists of the world including Van Gogh and Beethoven were addicts. But curing addiction does not lower creativity because your genes do not change. It is just your craving that goes away. So what really happens?

A study done on 96 undergraduates showed a reduction in the student's ability to do tasks that required visuospatial memory, when they experienced craving for chocolate. In other words, craving negatively affected the student's ability to remember.

Our bad habits cause craving which creates a distraction that makes it difficult to concentrate. When we need to concentrate we do our habits to eliminate the distraction caused by our craving. We give credit to our bad habits for helping us concentrate when it was responsible for the distraction to begin with. People without bad habits will not have problems with concentration because they don't experience the craving.

Over time people who believe that their bad habits help them concentrate begin to believe that it removes mental blocks. After you do your bad habits, your block will still exist, but only now you will get the job done just like how anybody would have done it. But your bad habits get the credit for helping you get the work done.

Your bad habits provide no mental performance advantage and believing it does is based on fallacy and myth.

Reward 4 - Confidence & Anxiety Relief

We acknowledge the relief provided by our bad habit as it removes the small amount of emptiness and insecurity. But we don't acknowledge that this emptiness and insecurity are the symptoms of our bad habits in the first placek.

People who have had their bad habits for many decades have been in a perpetual state of anxiety and emptiness so their bad habits seem to be the only way to get confidence and a relief from this feeling. Our bad habits do not relieve the anxiety in our lives, it causes it. People without bad habits never feel this insecurity or anxiety, to begin with.

Freedom from the self-loathing and dependency is one of the biggest positive changes people see in their lives when they break their habits. They are more relaxed and confident after breaking their bad habits and are better able to deal with their anxieties if it is not gone altogether.

Relief From Craving is The Only Reward

Craving and withdrawal can make you insecure, irritable, anxious or agitated. Though there is no physical pain, it causes mental agony giving us a feeling that something is not right. For example, smokers believe that withdrawal is a physical trauma caused by not satisfying their craving. But eight hours after putting out the last cigarette, a smoker is 97% nicotine-free. This happens every night during sleep. Only during the day does he feel the need to smoke every hour to fix his craving. After three days of not smoking, a smoker is 100% nicotine-free. Yet smokers relapse because of craving after months of abstinence. The truth is withdrawal and craving is almost always psychological even for smokers & alcoholics.

We associate our bad habits with pleasure because we see them satisfy our craving, but don't see them causing it. Our craving is not cured by our bad habits but is caused by it.

We might have started doing our bad habits for many reasons, but the only reason why we keeping doing them is to feed the craving. Every time we do our habit, the craving is satisfied temporarily. This provides a temporary relief, putting us in a normal state of mind.

But by doing our habit, we have set ourselves up to experience craving again in the future. The more we feed our craving, the more it takes to satisfy it. Smokers go from one cigarette to chain smoking fairly quickly.

What we really enjoy is not our bad habits but the feeling we get when our craving is satisfied. It is like putting on tight shoes just for the pleasure of taking them off. This is why by breaking bad habits, you are giving up nothing.

Hidden Drivers of Bad Habits

Alcoholics Anonymous (AA) have a concept called dry drunk, where alcoholics stop drinking but still remain angry, selfish and narcissistic. Our bad habits are often symptoms of some inner conflict. Things like anger, shame, loneliness, fear and hopelessness that makes people start doing their bad habits, needs to be addressed first. Until the flawed beliefs are fixed, we will always remain vulnerable to relapse. The habit of procrastination, for example, can be fixed only temporarily, if the underlying fear of failure is left unaddressed.

Bad habits are a way for our sub-conscious mind to avoid the real inner conflict that exists inside us. The inner conflict is either a bitter truth ("I am ashamed of my past") or a distorted assumption ("I screw up everything" or "I am better than everybody"). This inner conflict is never a mystery but we make it a mystery because acknowledging the truth is uncomfortable. It is easier to think we have no choice or control over our lives than it is to take responsibility for fixing it.

The best way to fix inner conflicts is through therapy which works by bringing our inner conflict to light causing them to vaporize like a vampire. The next best way is service. Helping others has helped AA members reduce their desire to drink. A study of 195 addicted adolescents showed that treatment showed substantial improvement when it was accompanied by service. 10 This works because love neutralizes shame and service to others reduce obsession and craving by eliminating the inner conflict. Helpfulness may not help break bad habits by itself, but it addresses the internal conflicts that create craving.

The System To Break Bad Habits

Now that we have addressed the core beliefs and issues that make us do our bad habits, let us look at the step by step system to break bad habits. With this system, you will be able to break any habit easily and effortlessly without using willpower.

Helping Others Break Bad Habits

Do not patronize the person you are trying to help, by telling them why their habits are bad. They already know this and don't do their bad habits for the reasons they shouldn't do it. They do their bad habits to feel normal.

Do not tell them breaking bad habits is easy as it will only irritate them. Give them the support and praise to keep them moving forward.

Do not force them to break their bad habits. Even if they try, they will use willpower to quit and end up failing. Tell them that people who succeeded in breaking their habits did not use willpower but instead addressed their flawed beliefs. Tell them how their bad habits only remove their need to do the habit which is perceived as pleasure by the brain. But in reality, their bad habit do not give them anything.

When they start believing that they can break their bad habits, their mind will begin to open up and that is when they are ready to read this book. Mention that there is no pressure to break their bad habits. If they want to continue to do their bad habits after reading this book, they can.

Where To Go From Here

The key to making it easy to break bad habits is to make your decision final and certain. Don't worry whether or not you have broken your bad habit. Know that you have. Do not ever doubt your decision. Celebrate it. Withdrawal is entirely psychological and if you are sulking, it only means you have not addressed your belief systems yet. Revisit Steps 2 to 4 in the system.

Don't make the mistake of procrastinating and not applying what you have learnt. You can wait for as long as you want to break your bad habits but the right time will never come and your habits are not going to be any easier to break tomorrow.

Some people think their bad habits has not caused any problem yet, so it is not a big deal if they don't break their habits now. The best time to fix the roof is when it is not raining. Don't wait for things to go wrong before you fix your bad habits. Break your bad habits now.

OBSESSIVE-COMPULSIVE DISORDER

Obsessions are more than thoughts we keep coming back to. They are constant, overriding all other thoughts, they are often impulsive and are typically inappropriate, forbidden socially or simply disgusting. These obsessions create a high level of anxiety and are referred to as "ego-alien" and "ego-dystonic" because they are typically completely out of character for the person dealing with them. The person will not be able to control the thoughts and may leave with a high level of fear that the thoughts will translate into an actual loss of control with the thoughts or impulses being acted out. Many people who are suffering from OCD may have irrational fears of germs or body fluids, or they could suffer from constant doubts that they have forgotten or overlooked something. The obsession might also center on a desire for things to be placed in or done in a certain order. They can also involve a fear of losing control, or the constant battle against impulses that are violent or sexual in nature.

When people suffering with OCD are faced with these obsessions and thoughts, they engage in compulsions to help ease the anxiety. The compulsions are repetitive, comforting behaviors or mental processes. Compulsions can be obvious and clear behaviors; such as checking, repetitive hand washing, or some other behavior. They can also be mental acts that are less obvious such as praying, reciting or counting. Compulsive rituals can consume many hours a day for some people. The rituals can be complex, taking up several hours; or several hours can be consumed on the repetitive tasks.

Some people are more neat and tidier than others naturally but someone who suffers with obsessive compulsive disorder takes neatness to the next step, to an extreme degree. A sufferer will spend many hours tidying, cleaning, checking and re-checking that objects are in order etc. to the point of it interfering with their everyday lives.

An obsession is a recurring thought, idea or image that although not making a lot of sense will continue to intrude on your mind. An example may be the thought of leaving your door unlocked, you recognize this fear as irrational but you cannot get it out of your mind, hence you repeatedly check and re-check that the door is locked.

A compulsion is the ritual you perform to dismiss the anxiety which has been brought on by the obsession. An example would be washing your hands continuously to dismiss the fear of being unclean or contaminated. You fully realize this ritual to be unreasonable but feel compelled to carry it out to ward off the anxiety associated with the compulsion.

Obsessions can occur independently of compulsions, it is thought that around 25 percent of sufferers will only struggle with obsessions, so the fear is there but they do not feel compelled to carry out the ritual to free themselves of the anxiety.

The most common of compulsions would be the hand washing ritual. You would be continually concerned about avoiding any contamination so much so you avoid coming into contact with anything associated with dirt or germs, an example here would be shaking hands with someone or even touching a door handle. You could literally spend hours washing hands to reduce your anxiety about contamination. It is thought that women are more likely to be compulsive about cleanliness but men would outnumber women when it comes to checking and re-checking items, as in the example of repeatedly checking if a door is locked.

It is common for obsessive compulsive disorder to first set in with males when they are in their teens to early twenties, and for females when they are first entering adulthood. The course of the disease can vary; but people can expect that the symptoms will become worse during periods of great stress. Certain disorders are commonly co-morbid with OCD; including major depressive disorder and generalized anxiety disorders. Roughly twenty to thirty percent of those people undergoing clinical trial for obsessive compulsive disorders report that they have previously experienced tics and another one-third of people suffering from OCD also have Tourette's disorder. Among people with Tourette's disorder, up to fifty percent of them will develop some form of obsessive compulsive disorder.

Obsessive-compulsive disorder is more often than not accompanied by depression and in some cases can also develop into phobic avoidance, for example, a sufferer will completely avoid public restrooms.

Obsessive-compulsive behavior was at one time considered a rare disorder but recent studies have shown that four or five percent of the world's population may suffer to a degree with this disorder. It is important for anyone who has obsessive-compulsive disorder to realize it has nothing whatsoever to do with being crazy or having a form of madness. You recognize that what you are doing is irrational and you are very frustrated that you cannot control your thoughts and actions.

Studies have shown that about half of all obsessive-compulsive disorders actually begin in childhood with the majority of the remaining cases developing in early adult life, a fairly small number of cases will appear in later life.

Obsessive compulsive disorder is clearly a genetic disorder that shows a higher level of familial specificity than many other anxiety disorders. First-degree relatives who have Tourette's disorder have a greater chance of developing obsessive compulsive disorder.

There are many mental disorders that can fall into the category of obsessive compulsive disorders such as trichotillomania (compulsive hair pulling), sexual behavior disorders, compulsive gambling and compulsive shoplifting. These other conditions are not as ritualistic as those commonly associated with obsessive compulsive disorder; however they do provide the same level of pleasure or gratification. Another disorder than can occur comorbidly with OCD is body dysmorphic disorder; with this disorder, the compulsive and obsessive behaviors will center very specifically around some feature of a person's appearance.

For some the thought of Obsessive Compulsive Disorder Symptoms may seem a little funny but for those suffering from the disease find the thoughts far from funny. It is reported that some 2.2 million people are diagnosed with this disorder every year. When you factor that some of these people have already suffered for a few years before seeking medical treatment their daily quality of life has suffered for some time with debilitating thoughts and crippling actions to their everyday routine. You may feel as though you are alone and that there is no one in the world that can help you, but I am here to tell you that there are thousands of people who have had OCD and beat it, including myself!

Obsessive Compulsive Disorder Symptoms -

Elaboration On Various Symptoms Of OCD

Obsessive compulsive disorder (OCD) consists of two parts. If you want to understand the symptoms of obsessive compulsive disorder, you should have the full understanding of both parts. The first part of OCD contains obsession while, the second part consists of compulsions. Now, I will separately elaborate both of the parts.

1) Obsessions. Obsessions are ill thoughts of a person with particular characteristics. These thoughts are not normal thoughts rather they are unwanted, penetrating and appear again and again in one's mind. This is the part which relates to mind of a person and, no other person can see it. Only the sufferer knows about his obsessions while, others may know through his overt behavior or verbalizations. Whenever these thoughts strike one's mind, they produce anxiety such as, the thought that one's hands are dirty. Whenever, this thought will come into one's mind, person will start feeling that his hands are dirty, and should be washed.

2) Compulsions. Compulsions are the repetitive, fixed-pattern behaviors. A person feels drive to perform these behaviors. We have seen that when obsessions come into one's mind, they produce anxiety. Thinking that one's hands are dirty, one gets anxious and feels compel to wash his hands in order to reduce that anxiety. Obsessions strike mind repeatedly, producing mental anxiety. As a consequence, person performs

particular behaviors repeatedly to get rid of anxiety.

Sometimes, people are over conscious about certain things. For example, there may be a person who is over conscious about his hygiene. He may wash his hands several times during a day. Psychologists diagnose obsessive compulsive disorder when these symptoms take the form of ritualistic behavior and, start interfering in daily functioning of the person. A person with obsessive compulsive disorder may get one or two hours late from office because he was busy in washing his hands.

There are different types of obsession such as, concern with germs, dreadful happenings (death, fire), perfectionism, religious concerns, lucky or unlucky numbers, sexual and aggression impulses and counting things. Compulsions may include excessive handwashing and bathing, checking (doors, locks, emergency brakes), touching, ordering/arranging things again and again, counting, cleaning households and miscellaneous rituals (writing, speaking, moving) etc. people may suffer from one or more symptoms of obsessive compulsive disorder simultaneously. Sufferers know that their thoughts are ill, and their behaviors are inappropriate. In some of the cases, children leave their schools, because their obsession regarding cleanliness compels to leave the classroom and go for handwashing.

Generally, sufferers think that their ritualistic behavior

(compulsions) will prevent them from obsessions. These compulsions reduce their mental anxiety for a brief period of time, but they keep on experiencing obsessions. Repetitive behaviors are observable in young normal children. Sometimes, it becomes difficult to distinguish between normal repetitive behavior and pure compulsive behavior. Usually it can be diagnosed when they grow older and, this is the time when their compulsions become firm. There is some difference between onset of the disorder among males and females. Males develop this disorder at an average age of nine whereas; females develop at an average at of eleven years. Moreover, children are more affected by compulsion whether; adults experience obsessions and compulsions at an equal base. The reason behind this may be that children are less likely to verbalize their mental processes and thoughts. Whatever the case, one should be vigilant about symptoms of obsessive compulsive disorder because, once they become fixed, they are most difficult to eliminate.

Obsessive Compulsive Disorder Causes - Elaboration On Various Causes Of OCD

Understanding the precipitating factors or causes of obsessive compulsive disorder (OCD) is essential because this disorder is most difficult to manage once it strikes an individual. Sometimes, there are some causes of disorders that can be controlled before the onset of the disorder. It is equally important to understand the various causes of a disorder because; causes are not same for all the sufferers. Management may be different for the sufferer who has adopted disorder from his family whereas, different for the one who has developed the same disorder after facing stressful family circumstances.

Obsessive compulsive disorder occurs at an early age and sometimes it is not differentiated from normal ritualistic behavior of the children. The disorder becomes obdurate till the time it is diagnosed. For such kinds of disorders, it is preferable to locate the causes of disorder for the sake of prevention.

There are different precipitating factors of OCD, and I will discuss each of them, separately.

1) Biological/Physiological Causes. Firstly, in most of the cases of obsessive compulsive disorder, we can find biological basis of the disorder. Empirical data has shown that individuals with OCD have first degree relatives with the same disorder. The idea of the biological basis of the disorder is strengthened by the co-morbidity of Tourette's syndrome and OCD which shows that the neurological factors which cause Tourette's syndrome, are involved in OCD, as well. Brain pictures of individuals suffering from OCD demonstrate abnormality in structure of basal ganglia. This is the brain structure which is located under cerebral cortex. Sometimes, antibodies react with strep cells and produce inflammation in cells of basal

ganglia. This reaction can produce obsessive compulsive symptoms in an individual.

According to researchers, worry circuit in the brain seems to be involved in causing obsessive compulsive disorder. Worry circuit is a set of neurons that produce signals of danger and warns an individual in anticipation of a threatening situation. It is hypothesized that this circuit consistently sends messages regarding threat and demands for urgent attention. This condition leads to obsession and compulsive behavior eventually. Serotonin is the neurotransmitter which is involved in obsessive compulsive behavior. Lower levels of serotonin in brain can produce obsessions and compulsions in an individual. This is all about biological or physiological causes of obsessive compulsive disorder.

2) Reinforcement. Negative reinforcement makes compulsive patterns stable. Individuals indulge in compulsive activities because these activities reduce their mental anxieties. Once, the individual know that carrying out some behavior will reduce his anxiety; he makes a habit to perform those behaviors. Psychologists from learning perspective strictly follow their views about the role of reinforcement in development of different disorders.

3) Social Causes. Element of prevention becomes significant when we talk about social causes. Some social factors have the potential to induce obsessions

and compulsions in an individual. For example, child sexual abuse is the factor that can produce obsessive compulsive behavior in an individual. Such children remain preoccupied with feelings of incest and try to clean their selves through repetitive bathing and handwashing. Parental neglect during childhood can also cause OCD. Any traumatic event that has potential to induce higher levels of anxiety, can be rated among causes of obsessive compulsive disorder.

Obsessive Compulsive Disorder Treatments

Obsessive compulsive disorder (OCD) treatments include a wide variety. Sometimes, clinicians (psychologists or psychiatrists) are unable to treat obsessions fully. In such situations, clinician tries to manage disorder as much as possible. In most cases, obsessions exist but, the patient learns to manage his anxiety, and prevents himself from indulging in compulsive or ritualistic behaviors.

Treating OCD takes time because obsessions are embedded in the mind and one finds it difficult to distract his mind. These obsessions produce anxiety. To reduce this anxiety, an individual performs compulsive behavior. Difficulties exist at two levels during treatment. Firstly, difficulty appears when an individual becomes habitual to reduce anxiety through compulsions. Secondly, difficulty appears when a clinician stops an individual to perform compulsion after occurrence of obsession.

Treatments for obsessive compulsive disorder includes a variety of techniques and therapies.

1) Pharmacological Treatment. Empirical researches have shown that neurotransmitter serotonin is involved in obsessive compulsive disorder. Low levels of serotonin can produce obsessions and compulsions in an individual. If this is the case, psychiatrists recommend Serotonin Reuptake Inhibitors. These inhibitors include Prozac, Paxil and Zoloft etc.

2) Psychotherapies. Different types of psychotherapies can be used for treating OCD.

The first thing, which a clinician can do, is to psychoeducate the sufferer and his family about the disorder. Psychoeducation consists of developing the full understanding regarding any psychological issue. When a clinician will psychoeducate someone about OCD, he will develop the full understanding of causes, symptoms and various treatment modes of disorder.

Clinicians widely use relaxation therapy as a treatment for obsessive compulsive disorder. In this kind of therapy, clinician teaches an individual to calm down himself. Self-talk or self-instruction is the technique which can be most beneficial for an individual with obsessive compulsive disorder. During self-talk, an individual talks to himself in order to guide. This self-talk is also helpful in preventing an individual from performing compulsions.

Treatments for obsessive compulsive disorder include family therapy. There are certain reasons for giving family therapy. Sufferer of obsessive compulsive disorder is already victimized in social gatherings for his repetitive behavior, but sometimes, family does not support its member, as well. During family sessions, family members of the sufferer are instructed to provide him social support and to empathize with the sufferer.

Exposure Response Prevention (ERP) is one of the most popular psychotherapies. In this therapy, the sufferer is exposed to anxiety provoking condition such as, the sufferer is asked to touch the handle of the door but, after that he is not allowed to wash his hands. In this way, his anxiety diminishes automatically, and sufferer learns that compulsive behaviors are not essential to reduce anxiety.

Hypnotism can be used to reduce symptoms of obsessive compulsive disorder. Hypnotist tries to reduce particular ritualistic behaviors through instructions. Cognitive therapy can be used for altering the meaning or interpretations of obsessions and compulsions. Mostly sufferers consider their obsessions as threatening that can cause harm for them. The task of the clinician is to challenge these obsessions and replace them with accurate thoughts. So all these therapies are included in the treatments for obsessive compulsive disorder and, these therapies can benefit a sufferer a lot.

PANIC DISORDER

Anxiety is a normal reaction that we all have when we are confronted with a stressful situation in our lives, but a panic disorder is a much more serious condition that can strike suddenly without any warning or reason. People with this disorder will have a panic attack which is a response to fear, however the response is normally out of proportion for the given situation. A person with a disorder will develop a fear overtime that they will have another panic attack. This constant fear of having another attack can eventually affect the daily functions and the overall quality of one's life. If not treated, having a disorder can ultimately rule your life. Normally serious conditions that include alcoholism, drug abuse or depression can greatly increase the probability that a person will develop a panic disorder.

People that suffer from a panic disorder experience a panic attack that can last around 10 minutes and even longer for more severe cases of panic disorders. When a person has a panic disorder and they suffer a panic attack, they often feel an intense and overwhelming feeling of terror, with difficulty breathing. A panic attack can also cause a pounding feeling in the chest and a dizziness feeling accompanied by a feeling that they may faint. Other symptoms can include sweating, nausea, and trembling or uncontrollable shaking. A panic attack can cause hot flashes or chills and a feeling of numbness or tingling. A panic disorder can be very dangerous if the proper treatment isn't sought. Experiencing a panic attack while behind the wheel of an automobile is not only scary, but can be dangerous. During a panic attack, a person my feel that they are losing control and that can be dangerous if that happens while driving.

Having a panic disorder can rule your life and make you very fearful to step outside of your door. One of the worst problems for people that have this disorder is the constant fear of suffering future panic attacks. Having this fear is how a disorder can easily start to rule your life. The fear of future attacks can cause a person to change many things in his or her daily routine, including avoiding certain places, situations and even driving or the willingness to travel because of that fear of having another panic attack.

An individual experiencing a panic attack feels an undeniable wave of fear for no particular reason at all. The individual heart begins to beat rapidly, his chest hurt and it became increasingly more difficult to breathe; at which time the individual believes he is having a heart attack and will die if he does not receive proper intervention.

One patient defined his symptoms in this way: I am so afraid; every time I start to go out I get that awful feeling in the pit of my stomach, and I am terrified that another panic attack is coming or that some other unknown terrible thing is going to happen to me or someone in my family."

Panic attack generally last no more than a few minutes, but it can be the most distressing condition that a human being can experience. Individuals who experienced one attack will have others. Those who experience repeated attacks, or feels heightened anxiety about having another attack are considered to have developed panic disorder.

Panic disorders are a serious health problem in the United States. Recent studies concluded that about three million people will experience panic attacks at some time during their lives. The symptom is strikingly different from other types of anxiety. Panic attacks are very sudden and often unexpected, seemingly unprovoked, and are often disabling.

When a person has sudden overwhelming fear and anxiety they are having what we call a panic attack (PA). The heart will pound and they find it hard to breath. They can feel dizzy and feel like they are going to vomit. Sometimes they feel like they will dye. If (PA) are not treated they can escalate into other problems and panic disorder. Severe cases can cause a person to withdraw from everyday activity. With treatment you can take control of your life once again and eliminate or reduce the symptoms.

Mary's story

Mary first had a (PA) about six months ago. When she had this attack she was in her office getting ready for an important meeting. Without any advanced notice she felt a very intense feeling of fear. After this she was feeling sick and felt as if she would vomit. Mary's heart was pounding and she was finding it hard to breath, her body was also shaking uncontrollably. After several moments the the attack had passed and she was feeling better. Mary became deeply worried about this as nothing like this had ever happened to her before.

About two weeks later Mary had her second (PA). From then on her attacks started happening more and more often. Mary is never sure when her next (PA) will come or where she will be. Out of a deep fear of having an attack while in public, Mary has been going home after work and staying there. Mary has also developed places she avoids such as elevators. She is not afraid of elevators just of having a (PA) while on one.

A (PA) can come on at any time without warning. Most of the time there is not a reason for the (PA). Panic attacks can even occur when you're relaxing or sleeping. (PA) can happen just one time or they can be something that happens repeatedly. Most people who suffer from (PA) have them repeatedly. Many times (PA) that are recurring, are triggered by a specific situation. These triggers can be things like high places, public speaking or riding in a car. This can be especially true if the situation has caused a (PA) in the past. Most of the time the (PA) comes on when you feel like you are in danger or cannot escape. You can have one or two panic attacks in your life and besides that you live a normal life. Sometimes (PA) can happen in association with panic disorder and depression. Whatever you may think, this is treatable. Many techniques have been developed to help deal with the symptoms.

Some of the symptoms of the onset of a panic attack

Most (PA) occur when you are not at home. You can have (PA) virtually anyplace - driving, at a party, taking a shower, at the grocery store.

The symptoms of a (PA) come on quickly and with very little warning. Most (PA) will be at their worst about ten minutes into them and be over in about twenty or thirty minutes. It is very rare for a (PA) to last more than one hour. A complete full panic attack can combine some or all the symptoms listed below.

- Hyperventilation or being short of breath
- Pounding or racing heart
- Pain or discomfort in the chest
- Shaking and trembling
- Feeling like you are choking
- Feeling like you are not connected or detached from your surroundings
- Perspiration

- Feeling like you are going to vomit
- Feeling lightheaded or faint
- Tingling sensations in your limbs
- Hot and / or cold flashes
- Afraid you could dye or losing control

A panic attack can feel like a heart attack.

Symptoms of a (PA) tend to be physical and sometimes these can be so bad, that people think they are having a heart attack. It is not uncommon for people who have panic attacks to make trips to the doctor, because they think they are having a heart attack. It is very important to have any possible problems checked out, but do not overlook the possibility of a panic attack.

Lots of people will experience a panic attack without ever having another one or any complications. Do not worry if you have had only one or two (PA). Be aware that if panic attacks persist you are most likely developing panic disorder. Panic disorder is having several, repeated panic attacks. Panic attacks combined with constant anxiety and changes in your behavior are most likely panic disorder.

Some Symptoms Of Panic Disorder

You have frequent, sudden and unexpected panic attacks that are not related to a specific situation.

You worry a lot about having more panic attacks.

You are changing your routine because of the panic attacks, such as avoiding place you had a panic attack in the past.

One panic attack can last only a couple minutes, but this one panic attack can leave a lasting negative impression on a person. Panic attacks that happen over and over can take a huge emotional toll on a person. Just the memory of the fear and overwhelming terror can hurt your self-esteem and create harmful disturbances in your life. This can lead to the panic disorder symptoms listed below.

Anticipatory anxiety - You feel anxious and tense between panic attacks. This is caused by the fear that you will have another attack.

Phobic avoidance - You avoid certain places and situations. You do this because you fear the place or situation will cause another panic attack. If you start avoiding places most the time, phobic can turn into agoraphobia.

Panic Disorder Causes

One approach to understanding the cause of panic disorder is that the body's normal alarm system the mental and physical mechanisms that allows a person to react to a threat, tends to be triggered unnecessarily, when there is no real danger in the immediate environment. Most medical studies are unable to explain exactly why this happens.

However, several psychological studies have showed, the root cause of panic disorder may begin on the emotional level or the physical side, or it could be both. The feeling of heightened-anxiety always begins with a trigger that initiates the fight or flight response from the limbic system. For example, the first hint of apparent danger your brain chemistry, blood hormones, and cellular metabolism all goes into action.

When you have a chronic anxiety disorder over time your anxiety symptoms may be triggered by less and less serious events because the limbic system has been sensitized to react in a highly panicky manner.

For example, if as a child you were constantly yelled at; as an adult you may feel anxious whenever there is potential for confrontation with an authority figure; and you may go to extreme measures to avoid such confrontation, even in a situation as benign as refusing a simple request by a family member or anyone of authority figure. At this point your conscious mind has lost track of the connection between your current feeling and your past emotional experience. You now have no idea why you are feeling panicky about something of so little significant.

No one knows exactly what the panic disorder causes are although there is evidence to suggest that it is the result of a combination of the following influences.

Genetics:

The chances are 8 times greater to develop this disorder if a family member, such as a parent or grandparent, also had it. Also, if one identical twin has it there is a 40% chance that the other twin will also get it.

Environmental/Social Factors:

Some panic disorder causes center around major stresses in life or in a person's upbringing. These include overprotective parents, parents who were always anxious, child abuse or some childhood trauma or high stress levels in the home, to name a few.

Other panic disorder causes may be attributed to the use of illegal drugs (cocaine, marijuana), drinking a lot of alcohol or caffeinated beverages, using certain medications that treat heart problems or asthma or ending the treatment of certain ailments like anxiety and sleeping disorders.

Medical Conditions:

Panic attacks can also be caused by other existing medical problems such as hyperthyroidism, certain heart problems, epilepsy and other seizure disorders as well as asthma.

Biological Factors:

There are a few theories here, one of which is that your fight or run reaction is triggered for no reason although researchers don't know why. Another theory is that when an imbalance of oxygen and carbon dioxide occurs in your system, a signal is sent out that you are going to suffocate which results in a state of panic. A third theory suggests the symptoms of a panic attack are caused by an imbalance of serotonin which is a chemical messenger in the brain that helps regulate anxiety.

Mode Of Treatments

There are a wide variety of treatments available for panic disorders, including several effective psycho pharmacology interventions, and specific forms of psychotherapy. Psychotherapy for panic disorder is equally important as drug intervention. Several studies shows that the combination of medication and psychotherapy treatment for panic disorder is more effective than either intervention alone.

Cognitive Behavioral Therapy (CBT) is widely accepted as the superior form of psychotherapy. CBT is designed to help those with panic disorder identify and decrease the irrational thoughts and behaviors that reinforce panic symptoms.

Psycho dynamic psychotherapy is another form of intervention that is seldom mentioned as an appropriate treatment for panic disorder. In fact, many therapist strongly reject the idea of using psycho dynamic techniques as an intervention to reduce the symptoms associated with panic disorder.

What set psycho dynamic therapists apart from the rest is their ability to recognize one indisputable fact: Panic states may, symptomatically, appear to be identical weather they are produce from a neurotic condition or from a manic-depressive state.

Clinical research indicated that neurotic type of panic states should be treated solely with psychotherapy; and manic-depressive states are to be treated with one of the many effective anti-depressive drugs. Proper differential diagnosis is the super-highway to symptom reduction for all psychological disorders, including panic disorder.

Treating Panic Disorder With Psycho Dynamic Techniques

Although studies have shown the effectiveness of cognitive-behavioral and psycho pharmacological treatments; many patients fail to respond positively to these interventions or have had persistence or recurrence of symptoms. Given the high costs and reappearance of panic disorder; there is a need to explore treatment options.

Psychoanalytic techniques are commonly used to treat panic disorder but have rarely been exposed to the rigor of scientific research procedures. Such a study would highlight and describe the psychoanalytic concepts involved in understanding panic disorder. While at the same time proposes a more "client-friendly" psycho dynamic psychotherapy for panic disorder called panic-focused psycho dynamic psychotherapy.

The potential benefit of this form of therapy is based on the belief that panic patients have a psychological vulnerability to panic disorder associated with personality disturbances, relationship problems, difficulties tolerating and defining inner emotional experiences, and unconscious conflicts about separation, anger and sexuality. Psycho dynamic psychotherapy focuses more, but not exclusively, on these impairments than other therapies, including psycho pharmacology, potentially reducing vulnerability to symptoms recurrence.

Unconscious emotions

According to psychoanalytic theory, panic symptoms are based at least in part on unconscious fantasies and affect In fact, both clinical and research observation suggests that panic patients have special difficulties with anger feelings and fantasies, such as wishes for revenge. These wishes often represent a threat to important love ones, especially those we have a close attachment to; therefore triggering a panic attack.

Patients are often unaware of the power of these affects and the revengeful fantasies that accompany them. Becoming aware, by bring them to consciousness, of this negative aspect of mental life and render them less threatening are important components of psycho dynamic psychotherapy.

Panic Disorder With Agoraphobia!

Panic disorder is at its most severe when it becomes panic disorder with agoraphobia. Panic disorder with agoraphobia creates such anxiety that a person will do anything to avoid being in what he or she considers 'unprotected space'. Public places are feared as 'unprotected' merely because a panic attack could happen there.

When a panic attack sufferer begins to avoid public places, agoraphobia has set in. The agoraphobic tries to stop attacks by making his or her world very small.

Agoraphobics have difficult networks of fears that totally control their lives. Major symptoms of agoraphobia are:

- Frequent intense panic attacks and severe anxiety.
- Avoiding attacks by staying home all the time.
- Depending too heavily on others.
- Never wanting to be alone.
- Avoiding any place where you can't escape.
- Fear you'll lose control in a public place.

- Feelings of detachment plus isolation.
- Helpless feelings.
- A persistent feeling of unreality.
- A feeling that your body is not quite real.
- Twitching, trembling, or emotional outbursts.

Agoraphobics have symptoms which are periodically disrupted by panic attacks. Agoraphobics have very intense panic attacks. Heart attacks and agoraphobic panic attacks look and feel very similar. The following symptoms are typical during a panic attack:

- Trouble breathing.
- Extreme disorientation or dizziness.
- Feeling like you may faint.
- Numbness plus tingling sensations.
- Blushing uncontrollably.
- Chest pain.
- Worry that you are dying.
- Thinking you are going crazy.
- Rapid pulse.
- A spike in blood pressure.

A disorder with agoraphobia is serious and will not got away on its own. Agoraphobia usually develops after years of panic issues.

The negative effects of panic disorder with agoraphobia come with social isolation, unemployment, and broken private relations. Panic disorder with agoraphobia can be successfully treated even though the symptoms are severe.

Early diagnosis is critical. Early treatment creates the fastest cure. Cognitive Behavioral Therapy (CBT) combined with systematic desensitization is the standard treatment for agoraphobia. Medication may also be prescribed.

CBT is a method for changing the way an agoraphobic thinks about fear and the world. Systematic desensitization actually desensitizes agoraphobics to fear so they never become afraid of specific stimuli.

Agoraphobics could start out by being asked to simply imagine leaving the house. When that can be done without panic, the next step might be to imagine opening the door. Stepping outside might be the final step. Agoraphobics are all different, but generally the prognosis for a full recovery is excellent.

Antidepressant medications may be prescribed to relieve the most intense symptoms. Drugs can improve the effectiveness of therapy. Agoraphobics may be weaned off medication when therapy is complete. Patients occasionally continue to take medications in order to maintain a full recovery.

Treating the panic problem early can prevent agoraphobia. The cause of panic disorder with agoraphobia is unknown. No other mental disorder is more common than anxiety and panic. Anxiety disorders are responsible for thirty percent of all the cash spent on mental illnesses.

Since panic disorder remains a major health problem in the United States it is important to continue to develop effective approach to its treatment. Panic-focused psycho dynamic psychotherapy will be a useful alternative or adjunct to cognitive-behavioral approach and medication. Psycho dynamic therapy addresses intra-psychic conflicts, defense mechanisms, and developmental issues not likely to be focused on in other therapeutic methods

Psycho dynamic approach also affect psychological factors that lead to vulnerability to recurrence panic state, or other difficulties connected with a panic disorder. A complete and randomized controlled trial should shed further light on the effectiveness of panic-focused psycho dynamic psychotherapy.

CONQUERING DEPRESSION

You know exercise, eating right, and engaging your mind are vital steps for a healthy, well-functioning brain. But how can you hit the gym when just getting out of bed seems like a monumental effort? Even cooking a healthy meal or tackling a simple crossword puzzle might seem overly ambitious for someone struggling with depression.

Depression, after all, alters the brain's chemistry in a way that reduces a person's energy level, lowers motivation, reduces the ability to sustain attention, and heightens the perception of pain. It may increase irritability or anxiety, making it hard for people to engage in social activities. Depression has even been shown to shrink the hippocampus, a key part of the brain that plays a vital role in memory and learning. As a result of these brain changes, depressed patients may experience memory lapses, sluggish thinking, or an inability to "connect the dots."

The exciting news is that for most people depression is highly treatable. And not just with medication. In addition to medication and therapy, there are a host of simple lifestyle changes that can help reduce the symptoms of depression and put you on the path to recovery. As a bonus, many of these changes have also been shown to improve brain fitness, leading to a brain that functions better now and well into old age.

The key for those suffering from depression is to start small and to recognize that every tiny step they take makes a real, measurable difference in their brain health. A five-minute walk, for example, might not seem like a boast-worthy accomplishment to a healthy person, but to someone who spends most of his day on the couch, it may be the first critical step on the path to better health. Of course, any lifestyle changes should be made under the watchful eye of a medical professional, so if you are depressed, or suspect you may be, be sure to talk to your doctor.

Nine things that can help you conquer depression

Get a checkup: this may seem like a no-brainer, especially if you've already been to your doctor for your diagnosis and treatment of depression, but many long-standing health conditions can contribute to reduced brain fitness, while not being the primary cause of your depression. Being overweight, for example, has been shown to reduce brain function and can contribute to depression. It may also lower your ability to exercise, robbing you of a key brain and mood-booster. High blood pressure, high cholesterol, diabetes, anemia, thyroid problems, concussions or other brain injuries, stroke and other health problems can all take a toll on brain fitness, as can low levels of Vitamins B12 and D, and testosterone (in men). Getting these conditions under control can help boost your brain, which in turn will put you in the best condition to bounce back from depression.

Check your medications: I often see patients who have no idea their medications are causing side effects. In particular, medications given for anxiety, insomnia, pain and even depression can cause mood changes, brain fog, or other cognitive and health problems, so it's a good idea to review your total medication list with your doctor to ensure they're not interfering unnecessarily with your brain function or health.

Sleep: Insomnia and sleep apnea, in particular, have been shown to reduce brain function, which can contribute to depression. Many people put up with sleep disorders and incorrectly assume they're untreatable. Not only are both conditions often treatable, but treatment can help reverse the damage done to the brain and lead to dramatic improvements in brain function. Diagnosis is easier than ever before – with a small device provided by your doctor you can do a sleep study in your own home.

Get moving: You no doubt know that exercise is good for the brain. Recent research has shown us that exercise can actually grow the hippocampus and improve brain function. Exercise is a also a tremendous mood booster and an invaluable tool in the treatment of depression. Depressed people may find the thought of exercise physically and mentally daunting, so always start small. Walk five minutes a day for four days, then add two minutes every other day until you're walking 30 minutes a day, five days a week.

Get connected: Depression can be socially isolating, but making a strong effort to socially engage is brain and mood-boosting on many levels. Taking a dance class, attending a spiritual gathering, or volunteering helps to engage parts of the brain that are vital for brain fitness. Even Skyping with a far-away grandchild can help kick the brain into gear and offer long-lasting cheer.

De-stress: Stress is a major brain drainer and can be both a contributor to depression and a byproduct of depression, so stress reduction is a worthwhile cause. Cognitive behavioral therapy and other therapies can help change unhealthy thinking patterns, while simple stress reducers can help you take some of the pressure out of your life. Set aside time to think about the stressors in your life and brainstorm ways to reduce them.

Be mindful: Meditation has been shown to help in the treatment of depression and has also been shown to boost brain function, even in healthy people. If you can't take a class, look online for tutorials on how to go it alone, or borrow a DVD from your library. If even that is too much, enlist the help of a friend or loved one to take the basic steps to get you started. Begin with just a few minutes of meditation or calm breathing a day and then work your way up to 20 minutes, several times a week. Yoga, and tai chi are other pursuits that may have mood and brain benefits and drumming therapy – which involves rhythmically banging on a drum – shows similar promise in helping people calm their mind and body.

Get thinking: Fascinating research in recent years has shown that the adult brain is malleable in ways we once didn't even imagine. Using your brain – by performing complex mental tasks – has been shown to boost brain health, which in turn can help you reduce the symptoms of depression. It's hard for a depressed person to muster the energy mental gymnastics require, so start by simply making an attempt each day to do something slightly mentally challenging – read the newspaper for 10 minutes, try to memorize five items on your grocery list, learn the names of three flowers that grow in your garden. Then aim to increase your daily "thinking time" each week.

Simple Ways To Overcome Depression And Sadness

Depression can be debilitating and is very different from just feeling unhappy. Depression is a pervasive feeling. It's almost as if you are in a black tunnel with no light. Hope disappears and the things you used to find enjoyable become a chore. Even winning the lottery would not snap someone out of depression and it is never a good idea to tell someone who is depressed to sort themselves out and pull themselves together. Unfortunately, it isn't that simple, but there are ways to alleviate the symptoms of depression.

1. *Practice Mindfulness:* a depressed mind tends to mull over all that is wrong and worries unnecessarily about all the negative possibilities that may emerge in the future. This negative thought cycle reinforces misery and is not helpful in managing to overcome depression. Mindfulness involves focusing on the present moment and is a skill that needs to be practiced. More often than not, our brains are full of thoughts and focusing on the present moment seems unnatural for our minds. Practice on engaging your senses in the moment. Focus on touch, taste, sight, sound and smell. Engaging the senses leaves less time for worry.

2. *Listen to Upbeat Music:* I have always thought of music as food for the soul. An upbeat tune can change an atmosphere instantly and create a more positive vibe. Listening to upbeat, happy music alters brain chemistry and can improve your mood.

3. *Use Touch:* science shows that touch therapies can help some people overcome depression, lower the stress hormone cortisol and increase the feel-good hormone oxytocin. Therapies to consider include acupuncture, acupressure, massage, reiki and reflexology.

4. *Include Omega 3 Fatty Acids in Your Diet:* research

has shown that depressed people often lack a fatty acid known as EPA. Participants in a 2002 study featured in the Archives of General Psychiatry took just a gram of fish oil each day and noticed a 50-percent decrease in symptoms such as anxiety, sleep disorders, unexplained feelings of sadness, suicidal thoughts, and decreased sex drive. Omega-3 fatty acids can also lower cholesterol and improve cardiovascular health..

5. *Stop the Negative Self Talk:* depressed people tend to see the world in a negative way. When things go wrong they blame themselves and when they go right, they put it down to luck. Depression reinforces self doubt and feelings of worthlessness. Monitor your inner negative talk and make allowances for this type of thinking by reminding yourself that your thinking is that of a depressed person, not a healthy functioning person. Don't take your thoughts seriously when you are feeling low. Acknowledge the thoughts but this doesn't mean you have to believe them. Keep perspective.

6. *Bide Your Time:* accept that your mental state is not entirely balanced. During depression, we tend to see the negatives in everything and find it harder to be balanced about what is going on. Gently remind yourself that you are tuned into the 'negativity channel' and don't listen to your thinking. It is definitely distorted when you are depressed. This idea alone can provide

some comfort when the world appears bleak. It won't last forever. Remind yourself that change is constant and that you won't always feel this way. Be patient and do your best to look after yourself in the meantime. Eat well and get a decent amount of sleep.

7. *Distract Yourself:* if possible, do your best to distract yourself from overthinking. Your thoughts are your enemy when depression sets in. Play with a pet or go for a walk. Read a book if you are able to concentrate, or finish a puzzle. Do anything that takes your mind off your fears and worries. Keeping busy is an effective way to overcome depression.

8. *Use More Light:* Seasonal Affective Disorder (SAD) is known for causing low mood over the winter months when there is less sunlight. Investing in a sunlamp – a 300 watt bulb within three feet for 20 minutes three times a day can help. SAD symptoms can include problems sleeping, anxiety, depression, irritability, fatigue, apathy and loss of libido. Using light can help to overcome depression and these other symptoms.

9. *Try Cognitive Therapy:* cognitive therapy can be extremely useful in counteracting depression and is based on the principle that certain ways of thinking can trigger certain health problems, such as depression. The counselor helps you to understand your current thought patterns and identify any harmful or false ideas and thoughts that you have that can trigger depression or make it worse. The aim is to change your ways of

thinking to avoid these ideas as well as help your thought patterns to be more realistic and helpful.

10. *Write in a Journal*: a journal can work in two ways. Use it to write down fears and worries. Sometimes, having an outlet in this way can be soothing and ease your mind. Another good way to use a journal is to write at least five things down every day that you are grateful for. This forces us to think more positively and can help to remind us that things are never that bad. In a gratitude journal, you can write about anything that happened in the day that made you feel appreciative. A stranger smiling at you, the sun shining..anything positive will do!

11. *Connect with Friends*: this can be one of the hardest things to do when feeling depressed, but it is one of the most rewarding activities. Force yourself to go out. Isolating oneself from others may seem a good idea, but put a limit on it and then get out there again. This can have a huge positive effect on your mood.

12. *Get Enough Sleep:* sleep and mood are closely connected. Inadequate sleep can cause irritability and stress, while healthy sleep can enhance well-being. Studies have shown that even partial sleep deprivation has a significant effect on mood.Taking steps to ensure adequate sleep will lead to improved mood and well-being. The quality of your sleep directly affects the quality of your waking life, including your mental sharpness, productivity, emotional balance, creativity,

physical vitality, and even your weight. No other activity delivers so many benefits with so little effort so aim for between 7.5 and 9 hours sleep per night.

13. *Forgive Others:* when we hold a grudge, we are the ones that feel the anger. The person whom we are angry with is probably merrily going about their business completely oblivious to your feelings. Don't allow others to have this power over you. They may have caused you grief in the past, try not to allow that grief to continue – it only affects you, not them. Lighten the emotional load and you will improve your mood and help you to overcome depression.

14. *Exercise:* regular exercise has benefits for helping to overcome depression. Exercise releases endorphins which improve natural immunity and improve mood. Besides lifting your mood, regular exercise offers other health benefits, such as lowering blood pressure, protecting against heart disease, cancer and boosting self-esteem. Experts advise getting half an hour to an hour of moderate exercise, such as brisk walking at least three to four times per week.

15. *Don't give up:* depression can make you want to hide away from the world and disappear. It's okay to take some time out, but give yourself a time limit and then do something productive to improve your mood. Depression can be well managed and there can be a wonderful life beyond depression. Hang in there and keep the faith.

HOW TO DEFINE A SPECIFIC GOAL TO WORK TOWARD OVER THE COURSE OF 6 WEEKS

Because of CBT's success, some of its tenants have become well-known. You might already have heard, for example, that thoughts affect feelings, or that behavioural change can affect negative thoughts.

But what other Cognitive Behavioral Therapy techniques and tools are there, and how do they help you? How are these CBT techniques used in a session?

AGENDA SETTING IN CBT

This is a collaborative process between your therapist and you to determine how to best make use of each session. At the start of each appointment both you and your therapist suggest items you'd like to discuss. A decision is then made on the order the points will be discussed, and how much time each one needs.

The point of agenda setting is to make sure that the session is well spent, and that the hour isn't lost to something that isn't of itself productive, like simply rehashing the events of the week. It is always a good idea to be thinking before your session about what you want to put on the agenda, so you don't walk away feeling something important was missed.

In the first few sessions your therapist will model for you how to set agendas. So you don't have to instantly feel comfortable enough to add items to the agenda yourself, but can learn over time. This is itself a valuable process, helping you take charge of your problems and their solutions.

GOAL-SETTING IN CBT

Again, this is a collaborative process designed to maintain structure and focus. The point is to make the goals for your therapy those that are relevant to you, with input from your therapist to make sure they are clear and are what you actually want as opposed to what you think you should want. Goal-setting makes CBT productive by highlighting the possibility of change, making insurmountable problems appear more manageable, and increasing your hope of overcoming them.

While there are many different approaches to goal setting, one of the more common techniques used by CBT therapists is the SMART way.

SMART goal setting creates a clear and vivid picture of your goal and helps you maintain your motivation for achieving it.
This is what the acronym stands for:

Specific: Avoid generalisation. Be clear and focused on exactly what you want. A specific goal has a much greater chance of being accomplished than a general goal.

Measurable: Establish concrete criteria for measuring progress toward the attainment of each goal you set. Ask yourself questions such as, "How much?" and "How many?" "How will I know when I have met my goal?"

Achievable: Make your goals attainable and feasible! How are you going to make this goal a reality? What can you do to make it more achievable?

Realistic: Is your goal realistic given your skills, time frame, etc? While setting high goals can be a great way of increasing motivation, it can also be disheartening when they are so high that you cannot reach them. This can leave you feeling like a failure.

Timely: Set realistic time-frames to avoid procrastination or giving up on your goal.

In pursuing your goals, if you find that that you are not able to complete a particular step along the path to your goal, take a closer look at it. It is possible that the step was too big, so do not be afraid to break it down further and go from there. It could also be that the step was not SMART from the start. See if you can rework it to make it one you can tackle.

Learning goal setting skills takes practice, but can be invaluable in helping you do those things you have been avoiding or "just don't seem to get to" and feel a sense of accomplishment. Consider consulting with a CBT therapist if you think therapy may be helpful for you in reaching your goals.

Understanding the importance of Goad setting

A lot a people who come for therapy it is usually because their relationships are suffering, and so they are suffering. It could be a teenaged boy whose severe social anxiety prevents him from spending time with his friends, a woman with depression that makes it hard to be the partner she wants to be, a father whose expressions of anger have put distance between him and his kids, or the college student whose alcohol-fueled behavior has alienated her friends. It's hard for our relationships to thrive when we're hurting.

Effective therapy can improve our relationships, whether or not those relationships are the specific target of the treatment. A relatively brief course of cognitive behavioral therapy (CBT)—which has been tested more than any other treatment—can lead to marked benefits not only for the person in therapy but for those close to that person. Some of the major relationship benefits of CBT include:

1. Greater presence. It's hard to overstate the

importance of our presence in a relationship, since we can't truly "relate" to someone who's not there. One of the biggest complaints about partners that I hear in my practice is that "s/he isn't there for me." Sometimes the person means quite literally that their partner is absent—always traveling for work, for example. Just as often the problem is that even when the person is there in body, his or her mind is elsewhere.

Mindfulness-based CBT can address both of these issues; for example, training in mindfulness has been shown in multiple studies to increase one's ability to attend to the person we're with (as described in this previous post). A CBT framework can help translate one's intention to be present into a plan of action to make it happen.

Try it: The next time your partner talks with you about something, bring your full attention to what they're saying. Practice seeing the person as though for the first time, really focusing on them and what they're saying.

2. Less anxiety. When we're overwhelmed by anxiety, we're not our best selves. It's no surprise that untreated anxiety disorders take a toll on our closest relationships. For example, the need for a "safety companion" in panic disorder and agoraphobia can lead to strain as the supporting partner has to adjust his or her schedule to accommodate the other person's travels. Similarly the chronic worry in generalized anxiety disorder frequently leads to tension and irritability, causing conflict between partners.

For any anxiety diagnosis, the treatments with the most evidence for their effectiveness come from CBT. The relief a person feels from a marked reduction in anxiety extends to greater harmony in the relationship.

Try it: If you've struggled with uncontrollable anxiety, consider looking into the best treatments for your condition on the website for Division 12 of the American Psychological Association. You can also search the therapist directory of PsychologyToday.com for a therapist who provides the treatment you're looking for. If a suitable therapist is not available, you might pursue self-guided CBT (such as with this book or my own workbook), which has been shown to be effective.

3. Improved mood. As with anxiety, untreated depression wears on couples. It's a struggle to be the partner we're capable of being when we have no energy, little enthusiasm even for activities we would normally enjoy, and no sex drive, among other symptoms. After a typical course of CBT for depression—12 to 16 weeks—the average person will not only feel substantially better but will be able to function much more effectively. And happier individuals make happier couples.

Try it: As with anxiety, you can search for a CBT

therapist through the PsychologyToday.com therapist directory. There is also evidence that self-guided CBT can be effective for treating depression (e.g., CBT in 7 Weeks or Cognitive Behavioural Therapy), so CBT is available even when a therapist is not. You can even do Internet-based CBT, such as this program.

4. Better sleep. As many as 23% of adults in the US suffered from bad sleep in the past month. When we're not sleeping well we tend to be cranky and impatient—not a recipe for the best interactions with the people who love us. Furthermore, insomnia can turn the bed into a place of worry and stress, which interferes with a cozy night's sleep beside our partner. CBT for insomnia (CBT-I) is typically 4 to 6 sessions and is the treatment of choice for insomnia. It helps a person fall asleep faster and sleep more soundly, and restores a strong association between the bed and sleep. And better sleep helps with pretty much everything.

Try it: If you've struggled with sleep, consult these guidelines for healthy sleep habits. The National Sleep Foundation has suggestions for finding a CBT-I therapist. CBT-I is also available through self-guided books (e.g., End the Insomnia Struggle) and apps.

5. Healthier relationship with alcohol. Problematic drinking can kill a relationship. Alcohol use disorder is tied to higher divorce rates, greater intimate partner violence, lower relationship satisfaction, and a host of other problems. CBT can effectively target the thoughts and behaviors that maintain problems with alcohol, and replace drinking with healthier ways of coping. Interestingly, the treatment with the strongest research evidence is Behavioral Couples Therapy, with both the patient and his or her partner actively involved in the treatment.

For many individuals with an alcohol use disorder, lifelong abstinence is necessary. However, there is modest support for a treatment program that includes the possibility of moderate alcohol consumption for some people.

Try it: If you're interested in learning more about the Moderate Drinking program, information is available here. You can also consult the PsychologyToday.com directory to find a therapist who provides Behavioral Couples Therapy for alcohol use disorders.

6. Happier kids. When a child is struggling with intense fears (e.g., phobias, obsessive-compulsive disorder), it can lead to tremendous stress for the family. Parents inevitably feel the strain when a child is refusing to go to school, struggling socially, or having problems at bedtime. As the saying goes, "You're only as happy as your least happy child."

Furthermore, most couples have somewhat different parenting styles, with one partner more lenient and the other more of the disciplinarian. A child's intense struggles will tend to amplify these differences, leading to conflict between the parents. At the end of the night when the kids are finally in bed and both parents just want to unwind, they may instead find themselves arguing about how best to help their child. Thus they may feel like their reserves are exhausted, with little left to give their child or each other.

The American Academy of Child and Adolescent Psychiatry recommends CBT as a first-line approach for treating many childhood conditions, including anxiety and OCD. Similarly, the American Academy of Sleep Medicine recommends behavioral treatments for sleep problems in infants and children, which can help both the child and the parents sleep through the night.

Try it: There are books available that detail how to apply the techniques of CBT to help your child with anxiety (e.g., Helping Your Anxious Child) or OCD (e.g., What to Do When Your Brain Gets Stuck). There are also many CBT-focused web resources available, such as from the International OCD Foundation and the Society of Clinical Child and Adolescent Psychology.

7. Healthier Thought Patterns. Even if we're not dealing with a diagnosable condition like anxiety, depression, insomnia, or a substance use disorder, the tools of CBT can have powerful effects on our relationships. CBT is based on an understanding of the connections among thoughts, feelings, and behaviors (see figure). When our thought patterns are aligned with reality, they generally lead to positive feelings and behaviors. However, when our thoughts become distorted in some way, they start to work against us, including in our relationships.

For example, we might notice that our partner left his clothes on the floor and think, "He expects me to pick up after him. He thinks I'm his maid." The result might include a fight driven by resentment and defensiveness. Or we could think that our partner seems distant and tell ourselves, "She's unhappy with me and our relationship," leading us to withdraw in turn.

The cognitive part of CBT encourages us first of all to notice the thoughts we're telling ourselves; oftentimes they happen so quickly and automatically that we don't even recognize the story our mind is creating. Once we've identified the thoughts we can test them out to see if they're accurate. Maybe our partner's clothes on the floor say nothing about his view of us, or expectations that we clean up his mess. And perhaps our partner's preoccupation has nothing to do with our relationship and everything to do with her worries about her ailing mother. With practice we can replace distorted and destructive thoughts with more accurate and constructive ones.

(Importantly, cognitive techniques are not about fooling ourselves or pretending things are better than they are. It would be important to know if our thoughts are actually valid so we can deal with the situation directly.)

Try it: The next time you're upset with your partner, write down the thoughts you notice and the emotions you feel. Then ask yourself the following questions (adapted from Retrain Your Brain: Cognitive Behavioral Therapy in 7 Weeks):

What is the evidence for my thought?

Is there evidence that contradicts my thought?

Based on the evidence, how accurate is the thought?

How could I modify this thought to make it fit better with reality?

8. Greater enactment of our intentions. All of us want to be the best significant other we can be. We want to be attentive, supportive, generous, patient. And like anything else, the road to impoverished relationships is paved with the best of intentions. If we're not deliberate about living out our values, we risk leaving them in the abstract—vague platitudes without substance.

For example, we might tell ourselves, "My family matters to me more than anything," and then live as though family is our last priority. We might idealize presence in our relationship yet attend more to our phone than to those around us.

The tools of CBT can help even when there is no "disorder"—when we simply want to commit to sustained action that supports our deepest values. It starts with taking an inventory of our relationship, and setting clearly defined goals based on what we find— for example, To listen when my spouse talks to me. It includes identifying specific behaviors we want to practice that will move us toward our goals.

We might plan, for instance, to turn off our phone during dinner and focus on our conversation. The goals and activities can be anything that's important to us in our relationship—we get to decide. It can be very beneficial to collaborate with our partner in the process by asking what they need more of from us.

A CBT approach also includes planning activities as specifically as possible so they stay on our radar, like putting "Come home early to make dinner" in our calendar, and protecting the time. Through daily practice of our intentions, we give our relationship the nourishment it needs not only to last but to be extraordinary.